PRAISE FOR FROM THE ALPS TO THE CASCADES

"Fascinating and touching. Lots of things clarified, lots of revelations for me!"

—Rhonda Peterson, environmental researcher, writer, and great granddaughter

"Wendy the Poetess has morphed into Wendy the Family Historian! Her family-history book, *From the Alps to the Cascades: The Story of the Stefani and Tinetti Families, from Austria and Italy to America* is a masterpiece of family history and history of the places her ancestors came from and went to. Wendy effortlessly intertwines remarkable and interesting stories of her ancestors with the history of the places in Europe where they came from, and the places they settled in America. It was a pleasure to read, and difficult to

i

set aside. Pictures of her ancestors and of some of their genealogical records (marriage certificates, christening records, even an Italian report card from 1877, etc.) helped Wendy make her ancestors "come alive" for me, and I loved learning about far-away places. Pick it up—but beware—you'll find it difficult to put down."

—Daniel Quillen, author of *Secrets of Tracing Your Ancestors* and *Quillen's Essentials of Genealogy* series

"*From the Alps to the Cascades* is not just another tale of the ever so important migration phenomena that laid the foundation of modern American society. It is much more than that, thanks to its perfect balance between historical facts and thorough reconstruction of the feelings and emotions that Frank and Angelina have experienced. It is a tale of two lives that intertwine through hard circumstances and joyful ones, all of that in a time that, albeit not so distant from ours, was remarkably different. Reading this book one can really understand what it meant to leave everything behind, not just poverty and famine, but friends and loved ones as well. All in all, it is a tale of an intimately human experience, it is not a novel nor an essay, but it merges the best aspects of both. From the first pages to the last, it is a journey, a very beautiful one indeed, through the lives of the generation that made America. Wendy, thanks to her hard work, gives everybody the opportunity to grasp a piece of history, and we should embrace it because it is a building block of our lives."

—Mario Agostino, cousin, chemist in Italy

"I love Wendy's approach to creating the book. It clearly comes through in her treatment of the many stories and in the way she presents them. Wendy's book is a labor of love and the tremendous behind-the-scenes work by her is apparent—labors guided by love and aesthetics—the point is that it shows."

—P. Rovinsky educator

FROM THE ALPS TO THE CASCADES

The Stefani and Tinetti Families
from Italy to America 1540-1953

Copyright © 2023 Wendy Negley

ISBN: 978-1-948261-75-3

Library of Congress Control Number: 2023923149

Cover & Interior Design:
Diane Woods: www.dianewoodsdesign.com

Published 2021 by Banyan Tree Press,
An imprint of Hugo House Publishers, Ltd.
Denver Colorado, Austin Texas

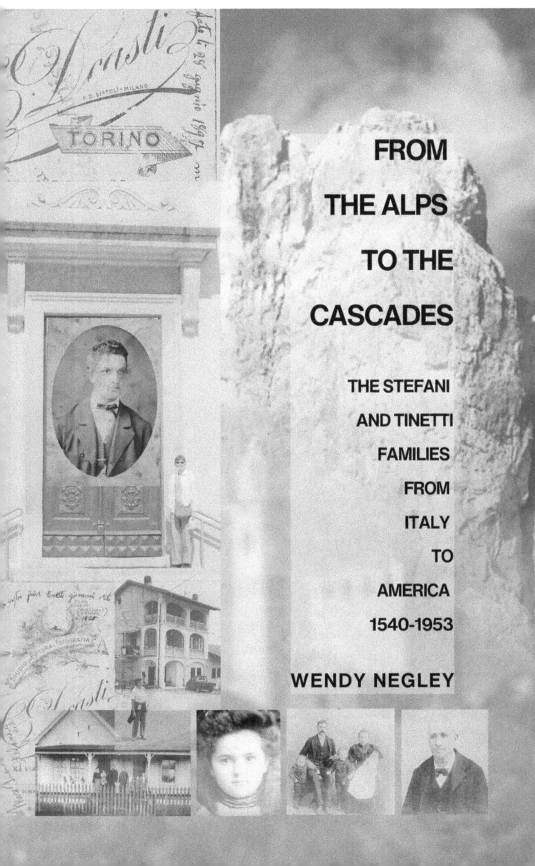

FROM

THE ALPS

TO THE

CASCADES

THE STEFANI
AND TINETTI
FAMILIES
FROM
ITALY
TO
AMERICA
1540-1953

WENDY NEGLEY

DEDICATION

To my mother, Margaret,

my sister, Rhonda, and my mother's cousin, Marian

Family Tree   *3 Sep 2021*

Names and dates

And places past

Just ink and dust

As dust they are at last

And yet I read the stories

Hidden in the tomes

My mind puts flesh

Back on the bones

The records show me

How they lived

This body breathes

Because they loved

They live again

Upon my tree

A kind of immortality

CONTENTS

Contents and Plates   viii

Foreword   xiii

Introduction   xv

A Note on Names   xviii

Chapter One: A Beginning and an Ending   1

Chapter Two: The Pale Mountains (Monti Pallidi)   5

Chapter Three: The Anauni   11

Chapter 4: The Stefani Family   17

Chapter 5: Life in Sporminore   23

Chapter Six: Sporminore in the Nineteenth
          Century, the Stefani Family   37

Chapter 7: Francesco Giovanni Stefani   49

Chapter 8: Francesco Comes to America   63

Chapter 9: A Miner in Michigan   71

Chapter 10: The Move to Comox, BC and On   83

Chapter 11: Life in Issaquah   89

Chapter 12: A Farmer at Last   101

Chapter 13: Life on the Farm   109

Chapter 14 Retirement: 119

Chapter 15: Fifty Years of Marriage   127

Chapter 16: Canavese   133

Chapter 17: The Tinetti Family   139

Chapter 18: Giovanni Tinetti   147

Chapter 19: Angelina   161

Chapter 20: A Portrait of Angelina
    by Her Granddaughter   169

Chapter 21: Letters from Angelina   181

Chapter 22: Frank's Last Days   187

Chapter 23: Final Words   197

Afterword: Return to Italy   201

Afterword 2   205

Afterword 3   223

Afterword 4   221

Afterword 5   223

Stefani Family Record using the NGSQ System   227

Tinetti Family Record   282

Selective Bibliography   327

Index   330

PLATES

1. FRANK AND ANGELINA — XIV

2. THE WERRA — XX

3. BRENTA DOLOMITES FROM SPORMINORE — 4

4. CIMA TOSA — 10

5. ITALY IN 1843 — 16

6. BAPTISM RECORD FOR GIOVANNI (JOANO) — 18

7. A VIEW OF SPORMINORE — 22

8. HOUSE 54 IN SPORMINORE — 36

9. FRANCESCO STEFANI REPORT CARD 25 APR 1877 — 48

10. FRANCESCO STEFANI IN PARIS AT AGE 18 — 56

11. CASTLE GARDEN AND NEW YORK CITY ABOUT 1800 — 62

12. ADELAIDE STEFANI CIRCA 1885 — 66

13. UPPER PENNINSULA MICHIGAN MINERS — 70

14. FRANK AND ANGELINA MARRIAGE CERTIFICATE — 75

15. FRANK STEFANI 1891 WEDDING PHOTO — 76

16. ANGELINA STEFANI 1891 WEDDING PHOTO — 16

17. COMOX, BRITISH COLUMBIA, CANADA — 82

18. GILMAN (ISSAQUAH) WASHINGTON, 1900 — 88

19. EDITH, FRED, MARY, ADELINA (DEL) — 90

20. FRANK AND THE LAUNDRY BUGGY CA. 1908 — 95

21. FRANK, ANGELINA, AND CHILDREN AT HILL STREET HOUSE — 96

22. STEFANI FAMILY 1918 — 100

23. STEFANI FARM CA 1935 — 108

24 FRANK STEFANI AGE 82, 1943 — 118

25 FRANK AND ANGELINA 50TH WEDDING ANNIVERSARY — 126

26 CANAVESE, TORRE BAIRO, AND TORRE CANAVESE — 132

27 VIA GIACOMO TINETTI IN SAN MARTINO CANAVESE — 138

28 PARISH BIRTH RECORD OF GUISEPPE TINETTI — 141

29 PHOTOGRAPH OF GIOVANNI TINETTI 28 JUN 1897 — 145

30 BACK OF CARD SENT TO ANGELINA IN 1904 — 146

31 THE GIOVANNI TINETTI HOUSE 2014 — 149

32 THE CHERRY TREE BEHIND THE TINETTI HOUSE — 150

33 ANGELINA (STANDING) WITH BONINO FAMILY — 160

34 FRANK, ANGELINA, CLEM, AND MARIAN — 168

35 MARGARET, ANGELINA, AND EDITH — 180

36 FRANK STEFANI — 186

37 MONICA REMONDINI — 196

38 COUSIN MARCO COLTRO, TORINO MAY (2014) — 200

39 TORINO — 204

40 FRIDLE FAMILY WITH VITTORIO, RHONDA, & WENDY — 208

41 MONICA REMONDINI — 220

42 SILVER STREET IN HURLEY, WISCONSIN — 222

43 CABIN IN PENCE BUILT BY MINERS FROM THE TYROL — 225

44 FERRUCIO STEFANI FAMILY TREE — 226

45 STEFANI -TINETTI FAMILY TREES — 232

46 WENDY WITH VALENTINA AND VALERIO RIGOTTI — 335

xi

FOREWORD

There are several people I want to acknowledge as without them this book couldn't have been written. I'll start with my mother, Margaret Edith Kells Peterson McDonald, who told me many stories of her family, introduced me to many of them and wrote down her reminiscences or those of others. She also recorded some family interviews which have been very helpful in writing this book. Second, my mother's cousin, Marian Stefani Hampton shared many family stories plus photographs and other memorabilia all of which were invaluable. Third, my sister, Rhonda took me on the trip to Italy where we were able to meet our cousins and see the places where Frank and Angelina came from. Unfortunately, none of these three are still living to see the final version of this book. (I did send Rhonda and Marian an earlier draft of it which they enjoyed.) Finally, my husband, Bill who was happy to make the extra trip to Michigan and Wisconsin while on our recent vacation so that we could explore another place from the lives of my great grandparents.

1 FRANK AND ANGELINA
WITH JOHN, FRED, AND EDITH,
1895 IN ISSAQUAH, WASHINGTON

INTRODUCTION

Growing up in Tennessee and Arkansas far away from my parents' families, I had a feeling of disorientation from my family heritage. Moving to my mother's home in Seattle at the age of 11 put me now in the midst of a large family of aunts, uncles and cousins. My mother was devoted to her family and she would take us to visit various relatives on a regular basis. Now I heard the stories and met the people I shared ancestry with. In the eighth grade we were assigned a project to find out about our families. This started me on a lifelong journey to discover my ancestry.

Rather than just noting names, dates and places as in a traditional scholarly family history book I decided to write the story of my Italian Great Grandparents. Many of their stories have been handed down in the family so this was not so difficult to do. The first half of the book is the narrative story of the Stefani and Tinetti family with the main emphasis on the lives of Frank and Angelina (Tinetti)

Stefani. The second half is the genealogical charts and family history. In this I have only given the Stefani and Tinetti line, although the charts include the families of the wives as known. Anyone wishing more data can contact me or view my public tree on Ancestry.com, called Stefani-Tinetti Tree.

To make the reading of the narrative story easier I have put the notes on sources at the end of each Chapter as *End notes*. As well, there are occasional footnotes which are comments or further data on the narrative and these are at the bottom of the page.

The line is taken only through some of the grandchildren of Frank and Angelina. I don't necessarily have full data on all the further descendants and this way there are a minimum of living people included. Again, anyone wanting more data or trying to determine where they fit in can contact me at wnegley@gmail.com or consult the tree on Ancestry.com.

I hope that you will be entertained and delighted by reading the story of Frank and Angelina and their families.

It is as American a story as all the many others written by the great grand-children of immigrants to this, our land.

Wendy Negley
San Francisco, California
25 Jan 2016

Revised: 28 Jan 2023
Beaverton, Oregon

A NOTE ON NAMES

The Catholic Church records are written in Latin and therefore the records usually note the Latin version of the parishioner's name. I have generally used the Italian form of the name as I feel that this is how the ancestor would have said it. Here is a list of names that have come up in the Latin, Italian and English form. Also, an ancestor may have changed the form of his name when he or she came to the U.S., not always to the English version of their name. I am including those as well plus nicknames.

Latin	Italian	English
Joannes	Giovanni, Zani	John
Jacobus	Jacobi, Giacomo	James, Jacob, Jake
Josephus	Josephi, Guiseppe	Joseph, Joe
Aloysius	Luigi	Louis
Martinus	Martino	Martin, Marty
Bartholomeus	Bartolomeo	Bartholomew, Bart
Franciscus	Francesco	Francis, Frank
Cristoforus	Cristoforo	Christopher, Chris
Maria	Maria	Mary
Dominicus, Dominici	Domenico	Dominic
Dominica	Domenica	Minnie
Catharina	Cattarina	Catherine (et al)
Margaretha	Margherita	Margaret
Carolus	Carlo	Charles, Carl, Chuck
Marcus	Marco	Mark
Petrus	Pietro	Peter
Antonius	Antonio	Anthony, Tony
Guglielmus	Guglielmo	William, Bill

2 THE WERRA

Chapter One:
A Beginning and an Ending

After being miserably ill for two weeks at sea, Francesco watched as his ship, the *Norddeutscher Lloyd* steamer "Werra," pulled into New York harbor.

Unlike later immigrants from Europe, he was not greeted by *Lady Liberty* and her torch. The statue had arrived from France only a month earlier. Her iron framework had been anchored to steel I-beams within the concrete pedestal built for her. Workers were now attaching sections of her "skin." Only a few such sections at her base would've been attached by 29 May 1886 when Francesco arrived. She must have looked like a huge skeleton rising above the harbor.

Soon—and not soon enough—he would be on dry land. He may well have sworn that he would never, ever, get on a ship again! But he had told Monica that he would come back for her. He had promised to marry and bring her to America. To make a life for her and their family together. That meant two more ocean voyages. Likely his gut wrenched just thinking about it. The ocean! (and likely he groaned at the thought.) But . . . Monica . . . and Sporminore . . . and the Pale Mountains . . .

3 BRENTA DOLOMITES FROM SPORMINORE

Chapter Two:
The Pale Mountains (Monti Pallidi)

Over two million years ago, most of Europe was at the bottom of an ocean. Imagine being a trilobite in this vast sea and suddenly huge cataclysmic changes occurring which thrust the bottom of the sea up 1000's of feet, creating the Alps. Suddenly you are in the mountains, not the ocean. This is what occurred about 65 million years ago. Fossils of such creatures are found regularly today in the Dolomite Mountains, part of the Eastern Alps. The land mass that is now Africa pressed up against the land mass that is now Europe, creating this huge range of mountains. The Dolomite Mountains are a special group of mountains within the Alps because they are made up of the mineral dolomite, a combination of calcium and magnesium, rather than limestone or other types of rock. This gives them a white color and until the French geologist, Deodat Dolomieu, studied them and isolated the mineral that formed them (named Dolomite for him) they were called the Pale Mountains. The name was changed sometime in the early Nineteenth Century, so it is likely that Frank Stefani called them *Dolomiti*, the Italian version of Dolomite.

The nature of their composition causes these mountains to take strange, phantasmagorical shapes. They often form spires. The Unesco site describes them thus: "vertical walls, sheer cliffs and a high density of narrow, deep and long valleys . . . Their dramatic vertical and pale-coloured peaks in a variety of distinctive sculptural forms, marked by steeples, pinnacles and rock walls..." The range called the Brenta Dolomites is in Western Trentino where Frank's village valley, the *Val di Non* is located. These are the mountains that Frank would have known, their highest peak, *Cima Tosa*, at 10,410 feet. These days, of course, they are a big tourist draw. But earlier they formed a barrier between the country of Italy and the Germanic countries to the north. Even so, into the fertile valleys, men came and claimed the area for their own.

End notes Chapter 2

www.italy-tours-in-nature.com/dolomites.html

www.facts-about-italy.com/dolomites-italy/

www.italy-tours-in-nature.com/geology-of-the dolomites.html/also see, "The birth of the Dolomites-Beautiful Mountains born out of the Sea" by David Bressan, Jun 13, 2012,

bog.scientificamerican.com/history-of-geology/2012/06/13/the-genesis-of-the-dolomites-

https://en.wikipedia.org/wiki/Deodat_Gratet_de_ Dolomieu

unesco.org/en/list/1237 The Dolomites

https://en.wikipedia.org/wiki/Brenta_group

4 CIMA TOSA

Chapter Three:
The Anauni

The earliest identifiable people that we know of in the *Val di Non* were a Celtic tribe known as the Anauni. The Celtic civilization covered most of Europe although in Italy it was only in the north. They were not literate and didn't leave any written history so we know of them mostly through the Romans who were busy conquering them; so Roman writings may be biased. However, in the last one hundred years many archaeological digs have turned up artifacts of these people which give us a picture of them and their culture. Of the Anauni specifically we know little, but burial sites and such found in Switzerland, Austria, and Bavaria of Celts around the same time suggest that Anaunians would have had a similar culture. We can date the Anauni as being in the Non Valley from the 6th Century BCE as Celtic bronze artifacts have been found at Sanzeno, a town in *Val di Non.*

The Celtic people in the Northern Italian area had a well-developed culture with a King of each tribe, a warrior class and an intellectual class consisting of Druids. The rest of the people were the farmers and workers. They made intricately decorated bronze vessels and jewelry as well as swords, spears and helmets. They valued horses and had carts with wheels. The women had a higher status than in Roman culture and there is evidence that they may have acted as warriors as well as the men.

In appearance the Celts were described as tall, powerfully built with blue eyes, blond or reddish hair, red being a particularly distinguishing characteristic. They had light skins, oval faces, and fresh complexions. They were a very clean people, using soap before the Romans did. They wore huge rectangular cloaks, pinned at the shoulder, woven in bright plaids, checks or stripes. They loved song, music and children.

We know of the Anauni through the Romans. In 1869, a plate or tabula was found at *Campi Neri* (Black Fields) near Cles in Val di Non. It is an edict by the Roman Emperor Claudius who gave the Anauni Roman Citizenship in 46 A.D. Trento was an important Roman outpost and many Anauni were already participating in Roman society (as stated in the edict). The Valley where they lived was called Anaunia or (in Italian) the Val di Non. It is called that today but it is still also referred to as Anaunia.

There is every reason to believe that the Anauni are the ancestors of the people who live in the Val di Non today. This area was never overrun by conquerors who intermarried with the population. They also have their own language, similar to Ladin, which is like Italian but not the same and not merely a dialect. Called Nones, one can see road signs in this language even today in the area. There are about 40,000 people in Val di Non who speak Nones. It is a combination of the Roman Latin and the Anauni Celtic.

End notes Chapter 3

Encyclopedia Treccani.it,
www.teccani.it/enciclopedia/anaunia
https://en.wikipedia.org/wiki/celts
Rauzi, Gian Maria, The Face of Trento Over the
Centuries, Curcu & Genovese, Trento, Italy, 2nd
edition February 2010, p14, 15 and 19
fsos.com/celtic_history.html
www.joellessacredgrove.com/Celtic/history.html
www.sacredtexts.com/neu/celt/micr/micr01.html
https://en.wikipedia.org/wiki/tabula_clesiana
Treccani, op. cit.
elalliance.org/projects/languages-of-italy/nones

5 ITALY IN 1843 SHOWING SPORMINORE, NEAR TRENTO
AND TORRE CANAVESE NEAR TURIN

Chapter 4
The Stefani Family

According to the book, *Sulle Sponde Dello Sporeggio* (*On the Banks of the Sporeggio*) by Pietro Micheli, Stefani, earlier written as de Stefen, di Stefan and de Stefanis, is one of the oldest families in Sporminore ("E' una delle famiglie piu antiche di Sporminore"). The name is from Stefano meaning "crown," and basically means descending from Steven. Today there are still Stefanis living in Sporminore.

The earliest Stefani ancestor of Frank's line for whom a record has been found in Sporminore is Bartolomeo Stefani. He is recorded in the parish records baptizing a daughter, Floriana, on 7 Feb 1563 and a son, Giovanni, on 6 Nov 1565. (Note the name Giovanni occurs very frequently in the Stefani line, he is the first of that name recorded.) This

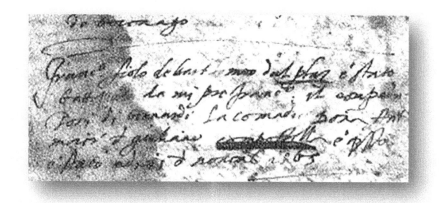

6 BAPTISM RECORD FOR GIOVANNI (JOANO)
SON OF BARTOLOMEO DI STEPHAN, **1565**

suggests a birth date for Bartolomeo of about 1540. The Council of Trent[1], meeting at Trento, established in 1560 that each parish priest should keep a record of the baptisms in the parish. The Pope so decreed in 1595. Sporminore being so close to Trento started keeping records right away so we have these 1563 and 1565 baptisms recorded. Bartolomeo's wife was Giovanna and that is all we know of her. Bartolomeo is the tenth generation of Stefani men from

---

[1] **Council of Trent**, (1545–63) 19th ecumenical council of the Roman Catholic Church, which made sweeping reforms and laid down dogma clarifying nearly all doctrines contested by the Protestants.   Encyclopedia Britannica

Sporminore who came before Francesco Giovanni Stefani or Frank Stefani. You can see the line in the charts at the end of the book. No more is known of most of them than their basic vital facts.

In about the year 1004, the Dukedom of Trent was entrusted to the Bishops of Trent and it became a Principality governed by the Bishop-Prince. As it was in the southern part of the area known as Tyrol, it was nominally under the Count of Tyrol and eventually the Archduke of Austria. In 1796, Napoleon occupied Trent but the Austrians managed to keep it as theirs. When French troops returned in 1801 the people of Trent rebelled and forced them to leave. In 1803 Austrian troops came to Trent and after 727 years the rule of the Bishop-Princes came to an end and Trent and its area of Trentino became a part of Austria. Other than these events life pretty much went on as usual for the people of Sporminore, including the Stefani family.

End notes Chapter 4

Micheli, Pietro, Sullo Sponde Dello Sporeggio p. 66
Chiesa Cattolica, Parrocchia di Sporminore
(Trento), Salt Lake City, Utah: Filmato dalla
Genealogical Society of Utah, 1986. Film/DGS
1388952, items 12-25 (Baptisms, Marriages and
Deaths, 1576-1923)

7 A VIEW OF SPORMINORE

Chapter 5:

Life in Sporminore

Sporminore is a small village on the top of a hill at the mouth of the Val di Non. It lies above the confluence of the river Sporeggio with the river Noce, which flows through the Non valley. In Italian, the word "noce" means walnut or walnut tree. Sporminore has a population of about 695 (563 in 1854) and has probably been around that number over the years. The name Spor was used to indicate all the cottages scattered along the river Sporeggio, the general term for the area. The area was called Spaurum when it is first mentioned as belonging to Gualtiero di Sporo in 1185. The Sporo or Spaur family were the Counts of the area from 1185 to about 1795. The ancient land divisions of the Spaur area were "Spormaggiore" (Spor major) and "Sporminore" (Spor minor) these became the names of the two towns,

Sporminore having broken off in 1200. Let us look at what life may have been like in Sporminore from about 1200 to 1800 CE.

Coming to the top of the hill you arrive at the town plaza, *Piazza Anaunia*. The houses were built of stone, sitting right next to each other and following up the hill. In front of the piazza was the original church, *Santa Maria dei Sette Dolori* (Saint Mary of the Seven Sorrows) with its cemetery.

The villagers would have had their animals stabled in the ground floor of the house and they lived above. Most people lived in the village and worked their plot of land outside of town, along the mountain side. The main crops grown were hay, wheat, corn, rye, barley, buckwheat, and potatoes. There was a family garden for vegetables. There were fruit trees. There were vineyards in Val di Non but it's not known if there were any in Sporminore. Local beers were brewed as well, following the Austrian traditions. The farmer had oxen or cows or horses or mules to draw his plow. The typical farmer would probably have a cow and a mule, and possibly sheep, pigs and chickens. There also were silk worms raised in the valley so that silk was produced.

The grains were cut with a hand sickle, gathered into sheaves and beaten by hand to separate the grain from the chaff. The separated grains were taken to the *mulino* (mill) where they were ground using water driven wheels, in use in the Tyrol from 800 AD. The barley was stripped of its core to make barley for *orzetto* (barley vegetable soup) or minestrone or roasted to make barley coffee. The wheat and rye were made into flour for bread and other uses. The women did most of the hay making in the family, it being used primarily for fodder for the animals. The grain may also have been traded within the Tyrol and with the Italian provinces of Lombardy and Veneto to the south.

Women were in charge of the family vegetable garden, cared for the feeding of the family, and did all the many household tasks of the family. They also were in charge of educating children in manners and in religious instruction. According to C. R. Brunelli writing in *Filo* magazine, in "Il Contadin," "Women were seen as the guardians of family tradition."

Marriages were mainly arranged by the parents with economic considerations paramount. The man and woman had some say, though. If a girl was interested in a young man, she would give him a bottle of wine. This signaled her interest. If the young man wanted a woman to be his bride, he would bring a bottle of wine and a glass. He would pour the wine and hand her the glass. If she drank the wine, it meant yes and they were engaged (pending the parental negotiations), if she refused to drink, it was no. If she was unsure, she would come up with excuses not to drink until she decided.

An engagement was confirmed at the priest's house with a handshake. The bride and groom with their fathers and godfathers would sign an official announcement of the marriage. Betrothal gifts were exchanged depending on the means of the families. The bride would give the groom something she had sewed and embroidered, such as a shirt or a handkerchief. The groom might give her a needle case or shuttle for her loom.

As Sporminore was a small town the young men would visit other nearby towns to find a bride. Frank's grandfather, Ferdinando Stefani, married Maddalena Conci from Taio (6 miles away) in 1820 and his grandfather on his mother's side, Luigi Paulino Wegher, married his bride, Elisabetta Fachini, of Vigo Meano (8 miles), in 1811. Frank's 2nd Great Grandfather, Cristofero Remondini married Margareta Franchetti from Taio in 1753. Her mother had been from Torbole (19 miles) when she married Giuseppe Franchetti in 1723. So, a young man might have to do a little traveling to find a bride.

An interesting family and social tradition was the *filo* (fee-LO). This was a gathering in the evening in the ground floor of the home. This would be warm with the fire in the stove plus the body warmth of the animals and people. There would be the smells of the animals, perhaps the barley coffee brewing and soup bubbling in its pot. The men would work on wood carving, the women would spin, sew or knit, children would play and listen as stories were told. Children's toys were usually wooden ones made by their fathers but included marbles and other games. Card games were also popular. And there might well have been singing.

Singing was very popular in *Val di Non*. It is said that if you have two Trentini, you have a choir! ("Due Trentini, un coro".) To the Trentini the preferred style of music was the choir. They sang and sang together at home working, in the fields working, at the *filo,* at weddings, at Christmas, at all other festivals, any occasion. There were love songs, work songs, folk songs, religious songs. Paolo Magagnotti, in *Filo Magazine*, says, "Song was embedded in the very blood and soul of our Tyrolean relatives. If you ask a Tyrolean what they do when three of them get together, their response is a right ready: we sing."

One may wonder about the food they ate. Polenta was such a staple of the diet that Trentini are often called "polentoni" (polenta eaters!). Polenta is made of grain, currently of corn meal. It is one of the oldest foods eaten in Italy, dating back to 990 BCE. Romans called it *polmentum.*

It was of Etruscan origin, made of various grains, it was adopted and spread throughout the empire. A Roman soldier used to receive a ration of grains called "puls" which he made in his helmet a "pulmentum." Centuries later, Thomas Jefferson served George Washington polenta which he had learned from a French mistress! It is made of corn meal, salt and water. The trio of Tyrolean cuisine, all of which would have been staples of diet in Sporminore, are polenta, canerdeli, and gnocchi.

Canerdeli is made of leftovers: stale bread, eggs, sausage, bacon, cheese, which are formed into balls and boiled in broth. It can be served in a bowl of broth or on a plate with a sauce. *Gnocchi* are dumplings made of potatoes, flour and eggs, formed into balls and boiled, then served with melted butter and grated cheese. There are, of course, many variations.

Tortei delle Patate (potato cake) was another key dish in Sporminore. The potato was the mainstay of the diet with the Trentinese preferring the Austrian variety called "sieglinde." Sausage, ham and sauerkraut were also common. With the potato, cabbage and cucumbers were the main vegetables. Relatively little meat was eaten, no red meat, but what was available was ham, sausages, deer, antelope and grouse, plus trout from the mountain streams. Trentino is famous for its red wines so these were drunk but so was beer (the Austrian influence.) *Acquavite* (Brandy) and *Grappa* were both made and enjoyed locally. Grappa is a liquor distilled from the stems, skins, etc. left over from wine making. It is a fiery liquor with 70 to 120 proof alcohol content. It was originally drunk mostly by the poor farmers to help keep warm in the winter. It goes back to ancient times in Trentino, now it is having a new popularity throughout Europe and the U.S.

In addition to what I've mentioned, other popular Trentino dishes that the people of Sporminore probably ate include: ravioli, macaroni pie, beans with salted meat, hare (rabbit), chicken (Trentino style chicken is stuffed with walnuts, pine nuts, bread soaked in milk, marrow, liver and egg), *probusti* (veal and pork sausages). For dessert, *pinza* (bread soaked in milk with sugar and figs) and *rosada* (almond cream). There are also cheeses that they would've made, probably goat cheese and *Trentino Grana.*

Religion was very important for the people of Sporminore. Their Church, *Santa Maria dei Sette Dolori,* would've regulated their lives with its church bells. Three times a day they would have bowed their heads and recited the angelus ("The angel of the Lord declared unto Mary, and she conceived of the Holy Ghost." in Latin!). In an article called 'A Catholic Utopia' written in 1886 for "Irish Ecclesiastical Record," Richard J. McHugh says, "The loyalty of the Tyrolese peasant to the Church has become proverbial. The Tyrolese Farmer never fails to lift his hat in passing a Church." The parish priest would've been an important figure in the lives of the people, both from his religious duties and as the most educated man in the parish.

One change that occurred in the lives of our Stefani family in Sporminore in 1774 was that of education. The Hapsburg ruler of Austria at the time, Maria Theresa of Austria, decreed that every child, male or female, was entitled to an education. And she ruled that every town had to provide schooling to all to the age of 12. So, the municipalities were obliged to do this and find teachers for them. Most rural villages adopted a one room school model. This made Tyrolean immigrants to America unusual as they were literate while 80% of Italians were illiterate at the time. Before this the only schooling would've been whatever the parish priest wanted to provide or private lessons of some sort. It's interesting that the only revolt ever fought in the Tyrol, fought by the farmers led by Andreas Hofer in 1805, was fought by men who had been educated thanks to the 1774 decree.

That was life in Sporminore from 1560 to 1800. But with the dawn of the Nineteenth Century, the winds of change were just around the corner and life would not be the same again[2].[3] [4]

---

[2] According to his granddaughter, Marian Stefani, Frank Stefani insisted on making the polenta in his household. He felt that no one else made it right! This may be because it requires quite a bit of strength to stir it as it cooks and it is stirred until the spoon stands straight up in the pan on its own. Also, the Val di Non version of Polenta and the Canavese. version may not have been exactly the same as each region of Italy has its own recipe for it.

[3] Frank Stefani is known to have enjoyed playing cards and the family often played. His daughter, Edith, played cards frequently with her sisters and friends and she taught her granddaughters to play Hearts, Gin Rummy, Pinochle, and her version of Solitaire. I have been accused of cheating at Solitaire and I reply that I am playing by my grandmother's rules!

[4] Frank's grandchildren by his daughter, Edith, were all singers, one of them, at least, even considered singing professionally. His granddaughter Doris sang Opera all her life. I have never heard of Frank singing, but somehow, he must have passed this Nonese tradition down in the family.

End notes Chapter 5

Micheli, op. cit. p. 53, 11

https://en.wikipedia.org/wiki/sporminore

Bartolini, Fabio, Belli, William e Rusconi, Tiziana; Sporminore, Segni e Memorie, Arti Grafiche Saturia, Trento, 2000, p. 16

www.commune.spormaggiore.tn.it/Territorio/Informazioni-utili/La_Storia_di_Spormaggiore

Bartolini, op. cit. p. 23

Bolognani, op. cit. p. 65

Brunelli, C. R. "Il Contadin", filo.tiroles.com/Customs.html

www.oldandsold.com/artiles25/marriage-customs-.shtml, "Marriage Customs of Tyrol and Switzerland"

filo, op. cit. Brunelli, C.R. "The Way They Were"

filo, op. cit. Music, "They Sang…Always…Together"

filo, op. cit. Recipes, "Tyrolean Polenta"

filo, op. cit. Recipes, "Our Food…Canederli"

filo, op. cit. Recipes, "Gnocchi"

filo, op. cit. Recipes, "Tortei delle Patate e dei Pomi"

Umberto, Raffaeli, Acquavite e Grappa Nell'uso e Nel Costume Trentino as reviewed at grapa.com/its/biblioteca_det.php/argomento-

acquavite_e_grappa_nell_uso_e_nel_costume_trent
ino/categoria=249

italiaoutdoorsfoodandwine.com/
indes.php/food_and_wine/
food/Trentino

fisheaters.com/forums/index.php?topic=2476011.0,
McHugh, Richard J. "A Catholic Utopia" Irish
Ecclesiastical Record, Third Ser Vol VII (1886) p.
742-748

Bolognani, op. cit. p. 69

https://www.culturatrentino.it/Temi/storia, "School
history and culture in Trentino"

8 HOUSE **54** IN SPORMINORE

Chapter Six:

Sporminore in the Nineteenth Century, the Stefani Family

In 1796 the winds of change brought Napoleon Bonaparte, at that time the Supreme General of the French Army, on his Italian campaign. He conquered his way across Northern Italy, until by the autumn of 1796 the French Army was up to Trento and advancing toward *Sudtirol* through the *Val di Cembra*. This is southeast of Sporminore and the *Val di Non*. *The Val di Cembra* had called a universal call to arms but this was mainly local farmers. Happily, they also had a local group of marksmen called the *Schutzen*. This was a group of sharpshooters who normally did things such as help out when there was a fire. The French outnumbered the Tyroleans by 5 to 1. Nonetheless, the valor and sharpshooting of the *Schutzen* managed to repel the French, who retreated. Four days of fierce fighting ended with the *Schutzen* forcing the French out of the entire Trentino area. There are many groups of *Schutzen* still today throughout Trentino who practice at the shooting range.

In 1800, however, Napoleon defeated the Austrian army. He put the Tyrol under his appointee in Bavaria. This rule was not loved by the Tyroleans and there was an armed revolt from the North Tyrol led by Andreas Hofer in 1809. Undoubtedly many men from Trentino joined in this fight but no data has been found of our Stefani men doing so. By 1815, Napoleon was defeated and the Austrians again controlled the Tyrol. The old Counts of Tyrol had died out and now the area was directly ruled by the Hapsburgs of Austria. The Bishopric of Trent was dissolved and Trentino was part of the County of Tyrol. This meant taxes and forced military service for the men of Trentino.

In Sporminore, life continued. On 11 Dec 1791, Ferdinando Stefani was born to Giovanni Stefani and Maria Catarina Remondini in House 54. They were from two of the oldest and most prominent Sporminore families. Pietro Micheli in *Sulle Sponde Dello Sporeggio* says that the Remondini family immigrated to Sporminore from "Ampez de Carnia" (Ampez in Carnia province, Friuli Giulia region) at the end of 1500 as weavers. Ferdinando was the second of seven children and the oldest son. In 1820, he married Maria Domenica Maddalena Conci da Vervo (Maddalena) from Torra, a *frazioni* (village) of Taio. This village was about 6 miles from Sporminore. Their son, Giovanni Luigi Stefani, was born 23 Mar 1821, also in house 54. Tragedy struck on 19 Oct 1822, when Ferdinando died of a malignant fever. Giovanni was 19 months old. What could Maddalena do? Her options were to live with her husband's family, but there were still young children at home there, or go home to her own father or remarry.

Maddalena remarried. On 10 February 1824, she married Giuseppe Weber of Mezzolombardo and moved there (a distance of 4.2 miles) to live with him. She had four children with Giuseppe. This means that Giovanni would've been raised by a stepfather in a village away from his grandparents, uncles, aunts and cousins. Giuseppe may've been good to him but undoubtedly, he favored his own children. One would imagine that as soon as he could, Giovanni would've returned to his home village. Or he would have done what young men in such situations have always done: joined the army.

According to Frank's son, Clement, Frank told him his father spent many years in the army. In those years Giovanni had learned to be "lazy, irresponsible, and dissolute." In the mid-nineteenth century, the military obligation to the Austro-Hungarian Empire was ten years. So, if Giovanni joined at the age of 18(1839) his obligation would have been over at age 28 (1849). This corresponds to the date of his marriage. These dates also correspond to the *Ten Years War* fought by Austria, under German domination, with the rest of Europe. Likely Giovanni fought in some of these battles. Perhaps he was glad to be able to return to his home village by 1849.

Apparently, he did so, as on 20 Oct 1849, at the age of 28, Giovanni married Elisabetta Maria Cattarina Wegher

(Maria) in Sporminore. Maria was the daughter of Luigi Wegher and Elisabetta Facchini. The Wegher family had come to Sporminore as blacksmiths in 1750 from a German-speaking town north of Sporminore called Laurein or Lauregno. The area they lived in was called Maso Milano, "Maso" meaning a rock or a boulder and "Milano" because a man from Milano had come there and started a blacksmith business in the 1500's. The Wegher family is still there today, running two restaurants and other businesses. Maria came from a more prosperous background than Giovanni and had a substantial dowry of goods and property.

Giovanni's and Maria's first son was born on 15 Aug 1850. He was named Giovanni Luigi Ferdinando both for his father and his grandfather. A daughter, Maria Elisabetta, named for her mother and her mother's mother, was born on 16 May 1852. She only lived seven weeks, dying on 8 July 1852 of convulsions. This must have been heart-breaking for both mother and father. The next daughter, Adelaide Maria was born 29 Aug 1853. She was followed by another son, Giacomo Giovanni, on 14 Jul 1855. Their daughter, Luigia

Maddalena, was born 3 Dec 1857 and named after her father and her mother's father (Luigi) and her father's mother, Maddalena. Luigia only lived seven months, dying on 3 Jul 1859. Exactly a year later a fourth daughter was born. Teresa Marianna, named for Maria's older sister, Teresa Maria Wegher, was born on 3 Jul 1860.

By the beginning of 1861, the family had grown to two sons and two daughters and Giovanni and Maria probably felt they were doing well. Unfortunately, that contentment was about to end. On 27 Jul 1861 their oldest son, Giovanni Luigi Ferdinando, known as Luigi, died of contusions ("contusione"). This means bruises and suggests that he fell or perhaps was hit by something heavy such as a falling rock. He was two weeks short of his eleventh birthday. This must have been a major blow to Giovanni in particular. His oldest son, named for him and his father, old enough to have been a real person to him, in whom he undoubtedly had invested many dreams for the future, was gone. What now?

More misfortune. Their daughter, Teresa Marianna, died on 8 Feb 1863. She was just over 18 months old.

Bouncing back from this tragedy, almost exactly 9 months later, a son, Giovanni Francesco (called Frank later in life) was born on 19 Nov 1863. Named Giovanni for his father and Francesco for his mother's brother, Giovanni Francesco Wegher, he was a healthy baby boy. Sometime during these years, their oldest daughter, Adelaide, had an accident and was bedridden for many years recovering. Fate had one more blow for the Stefani family, though, on 20 Jan 1867, when Francesco was just three years and two months old, his older brother, Giacomo, died. He was eleven years and six months old, older than his older brother Luigi had been when he died. This must have been another huge blow for Giovanni.

Individuals react to these sorts of tragedies in various ways. In Maria's case, perhaps she showered Giovanni Francesco with all her frustrated love and gratitude for his having lived. But in the case of Giovanni, he may have resented Giovanni Francesco for being alive when Luigi and Giacomo were not. He may have determined that he would not love his youngest in fear of losing yet another son and feeling he could not take that again. Given the fact that Frank always told his children how he had hated his father in all his stories of their relationship, we can suspect that such was Giovanni's reaction and that he likely hated his son as much as his son hated him. Francesco was the one who lived. Giovanni probably hated him for it and the more bright, alive, and capable Francesco was the more he would have hated and resented him. It's not rational but it's human and possible.[5] Now, how would that affect Francesco's childhood and life?

---

[5] Frank always said how awful his father was and how he hated him. When I researched the family, I realized that Giovanni's father's death when he was a baby, coupled with the deaths of so many of his children, may have made him an angry, resentful man. I felt this went a long way to explain his character, so I have written it here with that viewpoint, not to excuse his character flaws but to provide some understanding of the events which helped to create them. In retrospect we can perhaps show some sympathy for him and not paint him as a total monster.

End notes: Chapter 6

www.fabiovassallo.it/eng/cembravalley/sizeri.html

www.fabiovassallo.it/eng/cembravalley/battle.html

https://en.wikipedia.org/wiki/History_of_Tyrol

Chiesa Cattolica, Parrocchia di Sporminore (Trento), Salt Lake City, Utah: Filmato dalla Genealogical society of Utah, 1986. Film/DGS 1388952, items 12-25 (Baptisms, Marriages and Deaths, 1576-1923) item 15 image 774.970

Micheli, op. cit. p. 66

Chiesa Cattolica, op. cit.

Chiesa Cattolica, op. cit. image 01607

Chiesa Cattolica, op. cit. item 25 image 1178.485

Chiesa Cattolica, op. cit. item 21 image 1208.362

McDonald, Margaret, "Notes Concerning Frank Stefani's Early Life, as told by his son Clement", typewritten manuscript taken from personal interviews with Clement Stefani, ca. 1978

https://FamilySearch.org//learn/wiki/en/Austria_Military_Records, "Introduction"

Chiesa Cattolica, op. cit. item21 image 1019.734

Micheli, op. cit. p. 67

www.commune.sporminore.tn.it/Territorio/Luoghi-e-punti-di-interesse/cosa-puoi-visitare/Localita-Maso-Milano

Chiesa Cattolica, op. cit. image 01673

Chiesa Cattolica, op. cit. image 01677

Chiesa Cattolica, op. cit. item 25 image 1192.964

Chiesa Cattolica, op. cit. image 01682

Chiesa Cattolica, op. cit. image 01687

Chiesa Cattolica, op. cit. image

Chiesa Cattolica, op. cit.item 25 image 1192.964

Chiesa Cattolica, op. cit., image 01729

Chiesa Cattolica, op. cit.item 25 image 1193.762

Chiesa Cattolica, op. cit. item 25 image 1194.170

Chiesa Cattolica, op. cit. image 01736

Chiesa Cattolica, op. cit. item 25 image 1195.961

Certificato di licenziamento.

[handwritten] .... nato li 21 Agosto 1862 a .... nel *[handwritten]* .... di religione *cattolica* scolar.. della scuola *popolare di* .... di ..... class.. è intervenut.. .... all'istruzione per anni ...... ed ha riportat.. nei risultati dell'insegnamento la seguente classi-ficazione.

Condotta morale *[handwritten]* ....

Profitto:

Dottrina ....

Leggere *[handwritten]* ....

Grammatica *[handwritten]* buone ....

Ortografia *[handwritten]* buone ....

Comporre *[handwritten]* buone ....

Conti *[handwritten]* molte buone ....

Storia naturale *[handwritten]* buone ....

Fisica *[handwritten]* buone ....

Geografia *[handwritten]* molte buone ....

Storia *[handwritten]* bu... ....

Scrive.. ....

Disegno e forme geometriche ....

Canto ....

Ginnastica ....

Avendo quest.. scolar.. soddisfatto alle esigenze legali (§ 21 della legge 14 Maggio 1869), viene con questo certificato licenziat.. dalla scuola, ed esonerat.. dall'ulteriore frequentazione.

Dalla scuola *[handwritten]* .... in .... li 25 Aprile 1877

Graduazione delle note:

Frequentazione: Condotta morale:[1]   Profitto:

9 FRANK STEFANI REPORT CARD 25 APR 1877

Chapter 7:
Francesco Giovanni Stefani

Perhaps Francesco's hatred for his father even extended to his own given name. Although in his birth record in the parish book his name is recorded as Giovanni Francesco, it is never seen in that order after that. A possible explanation for that is that Francesco wanted to distance himself from his father as much as possible so took his middle name as his first and relegated his father's name as his own second. However, it also was the custom for people of the time to use one of their given names, not necessarily the first one. His mother was christened Elisabetta Maria Catterina, yet she was known as Maria. His oldest brother, Giovanni Luigi Ferdinando was called Luigi. At any rate, Francesco was called Francesco and not Giovanni.

As mentioned in the last chapter, Francesco felt that the Army years had taught his father to be "lazy, irresponsible and dissolute." He spent much of his time "idling, drinking, and chasing after women," but he still "expected to be waited upon." Francesco told this story to his son, Clement, in order to illustrate this: "Frank (Francesco) and his mother took care of the fire-wood supply by cutting down the trees, sawing and splitting the wood, and hauling it home. There they would find the father sitting by the fire. Being too lazy to add wood to the fire, he ordered Frank to do even that." This is just one of the reasons that Frank had little use for his father.

Giovanni operated at times as a peddler, selling needles, pins, small household items from his cart. He would take Francesco with him to pull the cart. The towns of *Val di Non* are located close to each other and would've been easy to travel to and through. Peddlers at the time often had a regular route and repeat customers. Francesco would pull the cart while his father called out for sales. Whenever he could manage to hide a penny in his pocket Francesco did so. His father would squander most of the money made (or so Francesco felt) so he felt justified in doing this. If Francesco's mother was sleeping when they returned, he would slip the money under her pillow so she would find it in the morning. This way he helped her provide for the family despite his father. She must have loved and appreciated her son!

Years later he told his daughter-in-law, Peechie Stefani, about his life in Sporminore. Peechie said, "he told me about his life in Italy. One day he told me that they had just a little piece of ground and each little section was planted in barley and corn and wheat and they had to raise that and take their grain that they got, their flour that they got out of the plantings, and that had to keep them. And for fuel, the government gave them a tree and they had to go cut the tree down, cut it all up for wood. And they even had to dig out the roots and cut up all the little branches - they couldn't leave anything - for fuel to burn in the fireplace. That's the only way they could heat their home. And he just thought it was a hard way to make a living."

In addition, Peechie added, "he knew how to raise silk worms, knew all about that. He worked with silk worms and he also herded goats in the mountains of Italy. And they would take the goats to the top of the mountain where they could graze and the man would be up there that would make all the milk into cheese. Then everybody would take their goats down when the pasture was gone and everybody would take their cheese home and that was part of their living for the winter."

Francesco's young life would have mostly consisted of working in the family fields, pulling his father's Peddler cart and going to school. In 1869, when Francesco was six, the Austrian Empire extended the compulsory education age to 14 years. The sixth, seventh and eighth grades were added. We know he completed this because we have his final report card, (Plate 9). This is his "Certificato di licenziamento" (Certificate of leaving school or graduation). "Stefani Francesco Giovanni born 21 August 1863 in Sporminore of Tirolo (Tyrol) of religion Cattolica (Catholic) scholar at school populare of Sporminore (public school of

Sporminore) of the 1st class of the period from 5 Novembre 1869 to 28 Aprile 1877, instruction to the year 8 (Eighth Grade) resulting in learning in the following classifications:

Moral Conduct (best translation I can get for his final grade is "agreeably pious or devout confirmed" which would seem to be a pass)

Doctrine: (illegible)

Reading: molto bueno (very good)

Grammar: bueno

Spelling: bueno

Composition: bueno

Arithmetic [1]: molto bueno

Natural History: bueno

Physics: bueno

Geography: molto bueno

History: bueno

Penmanship: bueno

Design and Geometric Shapes: bueno

Singing: bueno

Gymnastics: bueno

He received his certificate of graduation which says that he is relieved from further attendance on 28 April 1877.He would've been four months shy of his 14th birthday. Obviously, he was smart and a good student. If you look at the subjects studied, you can see that this was a pretty comprehensive education. His best subjects were reading, arithmetic and geography. After graduation (as many a young man has asked himself) what was next for Francesco?

Francesco left home to work and send money back to his mother. The family was very poor and he felt even one more mouth to feed was a burden on his mother as "she would feed the children and starve herself." He was thirteen but he looked older. Here is how his son, Clement, relates the story, "He left to seek work in more plentiful areas, taking with him only the clothes on his back; as he became hungry, he ate leaves off the trees. One day as he walked past another poor family's home he saw some cooked potatoes on the table, hunger tempted him, he grabbed one and ran. Though it satisfied his hunger temporarily, his conscience never let him forget that he had taken food from the mouths of another poor family that needed it as much as he did." Talking about this, he told his daughter-in-law, Peechie, "Even today," he said, "I feel so bad that I took that potato because they were so hungry in those countries, that they needed it just as bad as I did!" That bothered him right up to his last days, that he took that potato!

Peechie continued to relate what Frank had told her, "The nights were cold and he tells of sneaking into a barn one night to sleep in the hay and when the farmer came out with his dog, to check on the cows, the dog spotted him and barked and the farmer sicked the dog onto him. His ego was more hurt than his body, so again he had to start his wandering which took him into Germany where he found work in the steel mills and on the railroad. At thirteen {age incorrect, more likely fifteen} he moved on to Paris, France where he found work in a chemical plant making acid out of raw materials."

There was in fact, a heavy concentration of chemical industries in the suburbs of Paris starting in the 1840's. These were primarily for the textile industry but by the

1870's the metallurgy industry was rapidly growing and it needed chemical plants for such things as varnishes. Many immigrants came into the Paris suburbs to fill these unskilled jobs. It is interesting to note, that at this time (late 1870's, early 1880's), the Eiffel Tower was not yet built or even begun.

10 FRANCESCO STEFANI IN PARIS AT AGE **18**

So, Francesco's view of Paris was quite different from ours today. We have a photo of Francesco at the age of eighteen taken in Paris. He is neatly dressed and looks young yet his expression is one of such strong determination as to be striking. His hair appears to be a medium brown in this picture, it seems much darker in later ones. I believe that he was about 5'10" tall, based on the fact that in his WW II Draft record his son, Fred, is noted as 5'11" tall and in the Oct 1945 photo of the family Frank looks to be about an inch shorter than Fred. Of course, he may have shrunk an inch or two by that time so perhaps was 5'11" or even 6' when younger.

Clement goes on: "It (working in the chemical plant) was hard work for little pay. He lived on corn meal and potatoes with an occasional small fish or piece of cheese. He worked night and day sending most of his wages home to his mother to pay the mortgage on the farm so she would at least have a roof over her head. Frank became ill while working at the chemical plant in France and had to be sent to the hospital. His illness was diagnosed as a combination of the chemical reactions, over work, and a poor diet. He had been eating only salami and cornmeal so that he could send more money home. He was sent back home to recuperate where he stayed through the death of his father, Giovanni, on 1 Jun 1881."

End notes Chapter 7

Chiesa Cattolica op. cit. image 01736

Chiesa Cattolica op. cit. image 1203.238

Chiesa Cattolica op. cit. image 1193.762

McDonald, op. cit.

Fontaine, Laurence, "The Role of Peddling in Consumption in Modern Europe" p. 13

Factsreport.revues.org/3638#abstracts-en

McDonald, op. cit

https://www.cultura.trentino.it/Temi/Storia,

Bolognani op. cit. p. 69

Certificato di Licenziamento in possession of Mrs. Marian Hampton, Issaquah, Washington

Transcript on Interview with Peechie Stefani and Marian Hampton 13 Jul 1979

Gould, Virginia, Information on His Father, Frank John Stefani while Reminiscing with Clement Stefani – June 28, 1977, typewritten document, copy in possession of Wendy Negley

Smith, Michael Stephen The Emergence of Modern Business Enterprise in France 1800-1930, Harvard University Press, 2006, p. 222

https://en.wikipedia.org/wiki/Eiffel_Tower

Online publication - Provo, UT, USA: Ancestry.com Operations Inc, 2005.Original data - United States, Selective Service System. World War I Selective Service System Draft Registration Cards, 1917-1918. Washington, D.C.: National Archives and Records Administration image 1691

Gould, op. cit.

"Italia, Trento, Diocesi di Trento, Registri Parrocchiali, 1548-1937," database with images,

FamilySearch (https://familysearch.org/ark:/61903/1:1:XVYS-NSQ : accessed 21 January 2016), Cunegonda Monica Remondini, 02 Feb 1869, Baptism; citing p. 32, Santa Maria Addolorata, Sporminore, Trento, Italy, Archdiocesi di Trento, Trento (Archdiocese of Trento, Trento); FHL microfilm 1,388,952. image 01751

Transcript 13 Jul 1079, op. cit.

Reise-Pass – Passaporto issued to Francesco Stefani Feb 1882, in possession of Mrs. Marian Hampton of Issaquah, Washington

Reid, op. cit.

King Co., Washington, Naturalization papers 15 Oct 1894, Journal 4, p. 22

Ancestry, U.S. Federal Census 1900 Gilman, King, Washington, Roll T623-1744, p. 2A, ED 74, family 23, says 1885,

Ancestry, U.S. Federal Census 1920 Issaquah, King, Washington, T625_1924, p. 1B, ED 39, Family 20, says 1888

Ancestry, U.S. Federal Census 1930 Gilman, King, Washington, Roll 2490, p.2B, ED 285, Image 1430 Family 43, says 1885

Ancestry, Year: 1886 Arrival: New York Microfilm Serial: M237, 1820-1897, Microfilm Roll 495, Line 34, List Number 607, image 98; Ship Werra from Bremen arrived 29 May 1886, Joh Stefani, b. 1861, Male, Austrian

Gould, op. cit.

Chiesa Cattolica, op. cit. ite3m 25 image 1203.238

11 CASTLE GARDEN AND NEW YORK CITY ABOUT 1880

Chapter 8:

Francesco Comes to America

First let us ask ourselves, why would a man leave the town where his family had lived for over 300 years, leaving the only family and friends he had ever known, to go to an unknown land with a different language, customs, life? Yet in the years 1870 to 1888, 61 people immigrated to the United States from Sporminore, a town with a population of only about 550. Asking why, we find the following: In the best of times, it was a struggle to eke a living out of the small plots of land assigned to the peasant farmers and carved out of the rocky hillsides. In 1882 and 1885 severe natural disasters added to the difficulties. There was major flooding and new and difficult plant diseases affecting their main staple crops. As a result, the people starved.

In addition, the *Risorgimento* (Unification of Italy of 1864) had removed Trentino's neighbors, Lombardy and Veneto, from Austria. These were the main trading partners for Trentino but now to trade with them meant paying customs duties. On top of this, inoculation for Small Pox had increased the population so there were more mouths to feed. Opportunities for work were rare, wages were low when one could find work and industry was obsolete and depressed. It was not a scene which offered a future to a young man with ambition.

The people of *Val di Non* had long engaged in seasonal emigration to other countries in Europe to take part in harvests, work as chimney sweeps and other jobs, much as Francesco had done in Germany, France and Alsace. So many of the immigrants to America planned to return, in fact this was quite common with Italian Immigrants in the 20th Century who were called "birds of passage" for their frequent trips back and forth. But this was not so common with the men of Sporminore.

Talking to his daughter-in-law, Peechie, Frank said this about why he decided to go to America: "He told me it was such a hard time in Italy that he always did want to leave there and when he was about, I believe he said, 28 years old, he decided to leave. And they all hear about America, the Land of Opportunity. So, he came here."

By about 1885, Francesco was engaged to Monica Remondini. He was 22 and she was 16. He planned to go to America, establish himself, and return for her. They would get married and then go to America together to live. Francesco's mother, Maria, died in November 1884. He turned the house and all other affairs over to his sister, Adelaide. She was engaged to Federico Friedle although they didn't marry until 1887. At any rate, he probably felt that she was well provided for thus, enabling him to board a ship and arrive in New York in May 1885 (or 1886 as per the passenger list which seems to show him on it).

12 ADELAIDE STEFANI CIRCA **1885**

What was the trip like? Bonifacio Bolognani in his
book, *A Courageous People from the Dolomites*, describes it
this way:

"Those who left Trentino went to Trent by jolting
cart (Francesco may well have walked instead). At the
window of the *Gottardi Agency* they bought tickets for 500
crowns which included boat fare and the first expenses in the
United States. Tickets for passage from Le Havre or

Hamburg (or Bremen which is where Francesco probably traveled from) to New York City cost $15 in 1880, $28 in 1900.

"For that amount of money, the poor emigrant was forced to go down into the bottom of the steamship, in a dark room with a row of wooden shelves where both men and women slept. At the ringing of a bell, all stood in line with a tin plate bought at port to wait for soup and a piece of bread. The life on board ship was made miserable by storms, sea sickness and strong odours. The trip on a low tonnage boat took 15 to 25 days, according to conditions at sea. The food was scarce and ill cooked. "

Francesco had a harder time on the voyage than many because he was constantly seasick, probably rarely getting out of his shelf bed. It was a horrendous journey and he vowed never to travel by sea again.

Upon arrival in New York City, Francesco would have disembarked at *Castle Garden* at the southern tip of Manhattan. Here he would have presented his Austrian passport which would have gotten him admitted easily as opposed to an Italian one (the Italians were less desirable to the Americans at the time). He would have had correspondence with friends or relatives working in the mines in Michigan and likely gotten immediately onto a train for the Upper Peninsula. It is likely that he knew men working in the mines as we find men from Sporminore in the records there.

As I have said, the *Statue of Liberty* was under construction when Francesco arrived. Thus, he would not have shared the experience of so many later immigrants. But Francesco had come to America, what would this mean to him?

End notes Chapter 8

Bolognani, op. cit. p. 174

The *Filo*, "Immigration History", Groselli, Renzo M., "La Miseria",

filo.tiroles.com/immigrationhistory.html

Bolognani, op. cit. p. 171

The *Filo*, op. cit. "Immigration History" "the History of Our Immigration"

www.digitalhistory.uh.edu/disp-textbook.cfm?smtID=2&psid=3290 "birds of passage"

McDonald, op. cit.; Gould op. cit.

Chiesa Cattolica, op. cit. item 25 image 1203.238

Chiesa Cattolica, op. cit. item 22 image 1059.301

Ancestry Year: 1886, op. cit.

Bolognani, op. cit. p. 193

Bolognani, op. cit. p.194

https://en.wikipedia.org/wiki/Statue_of_Liberty

13 UPPER PENNINSULA MICHIGAN MINERS

ABOUT THE TIME FRANK WAS THERE

Chapter 9:

A Miner in Michigan

Iron ore was discovered in the Upper Peninsula of Michigan in 1844 but it couldn't really be profitably mined until the railroads arrived to the area. In the Menominee Range iron mines were established in the towns of Norway and Vulcan by 1877. The Iron mining companies looking for workers advertised in Europe, in the Slavic countries, Finland, Sweden and Austro-Hungary. The men of Sporminore would have seen these ads. In fact, it is highly likely that Frank (since he is in America now, we will call him Frank, however, the records we have from Michigan still call him Francesco, by Issaquah he is Frank in all records) knew men already working in these mines and he was simply joining them. In fact, on 2 Apr 1888 when Frank declared his intention to become an American citizen five other men who

71

have common Sporminore surnames also did so. Two had arrived before Frank and three after. On the same page with Frank is his cousin, Alfonzo Wegher, the son of his mother's brother, Celeste. Alfonzo left his wife and two daughters behind in Sporminore. Then it seems that he returned to them in 1890 as more births start being recorded in the Sporminore parish record in 1891. At any rate, Frank went to work with fellow countrymen when he first arrived.

Family lore is that he first lived in Norway, Michigan. There were several mines there or nearby that he could have worked at. They were much alike. According to Bolognani, "The iron miners worked ten hours a day, reaching depths of 2,000 feet and earned only $1.60 a day." The average U.S. income in 1880 was only $1.00 a day, a factory worker was making $1.48 a day, so actually the miners were earning above average pay. Which explains why anyone would do it.

Norway had little to offer as a town, there was a Post Office there beginning in 1891. Frank moved from there to the town of Iron Mountain, another small mining town. The town of Hurley, Wisconsin was bigger and was just across the river. It was here that Frank went to the Saloon owned and operated by Rosa and Luigi Bonino. They came to Hurley in 1889 and were from the Piedmont area of Northern Italy. Frank probably liked them and could speak Italian with them. They had two daughters when they arrived and a son was born in 1891. Rosa had brought her twin sister, Minnie, over from Italy in 1888 to marry one of the miners in Illinois, so Frank probably would have heard about that. Frank undoubtedly was feeling the need of a wife.

When Frank came to America he was engaged to Monica Remondini as we have covered. However, on the ship from Europe to America Frank was so sick and miserable that he just couldn't face doing the passage again. The plan had been that he would return and marry Monica and then bring her to America. But he couldn't see himself doing that (two more ocean crossings!). So, he wrote to her and told her he released her from the engagement and why. Apparently, she accepted this and couldn't see herself coming to America without him, as she married Frank's cousin, Guilio Wegher, on 14 Apr 1888, 12 days after Frank filed his *Declaration of Intention* to become a citizen. Guilio was the son of another of Frank's mother's brothers, Guilio Fortunato Wegher. He and Monica had eight children. Monica died in 1931 in Sporminore, her grave can still be seen there.

Thus, Frank needed a wife. He asked Rosa if she had any more sisters at home. He proposed that he would pay her sister's passage to America and if the sister didn't want to marry him (or vice versa) he would pay her passage back to Italy. Rosa was reluctant because she felt that Minnie's marriage hadn't gone well (although, actually Minnie and her husband were married for the rest of their lives, had many children and descendants, so it was successful). But Frank talked her into it. So, she sent for her younger sister, Angelina, who came in 1890. (There was another sister between Rosa and Angelina in age, Albina, perhaps she didn't want to come or was already married.)

Frank and Angelina hit it off. They were married on 2 Jun 1891 in Hurley. [6] [7]

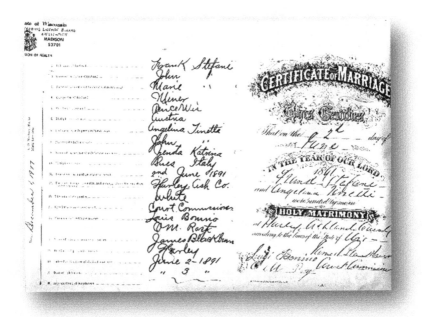

14 FRANK AND ANGELINA MARRIAGE CERTIFICATE

---

[6] Luigi and Rosa were their witnesses. Angelina wore a lavender dress with a fur collar. We have the photo. Frank was making enough to support a wife and now he had a wife. Things were starting to come together.

[7] I have been given two versions of how Frank and Angelina met. The one above is from Ruth Marcotte, granddaughter of Rosa Tinetti Bonino. Ruth was told that Angelina's family didn't know this story. The account I was told by my family is different and I will tell that version when I tell Angelina's story.

15 FRANK STEFANI **1891** WEDDING PHOTO

16 ANGELINA STEFANI **1891** WEDDING PHOTO

End notes Chapter 9

Bolognani, op. cit. p. 248-249

Dickinson County Michigan Genealogy, "Norway" and "Vulcan Mine" dickinson.genwebsite.net

gogebicroots.com/history.aspx

Family Search, Wisconsin County Naturalization Records 1807-1992, Ashland Co., Declarations of Intentions 1884-1888, vol. 2, p. 466, image 468

"Italia, Trento, Diocesi di Trento, Registri Parrocchiali, 1548-1937," database with images, *FamilySearch* (https://familysearch.org/ark:/61903/1:1:XVYS-852 : accessed 5 January 2016), Alfonso Eugenio Celeste Wegher, 16 Aug 1857, Baptism; citing p. 1, Santa Maria Addolorata, Sporminore, Trento, Italy, Archdiocesi di Trento, Trento (Archdiocese of Trento, Trento); FHL microfilm 1,388,952. Image 01720.

"Italia, Trento, Diocesi di Trento, Registri Parrocchiali, 1548-1937," database with images,*FamilySearch* (https://familysearch.org/ark:/61903/1:1:XVYS-LZJ : accessed 5 January 2016), Alfonso Wegher in entry for Celestina Maria Luigia Wegher, 23 Nov 1882, Baptism; citing p. 73, Santa Maria Addolorata, Sporminore, Trento, Italy, Archdiocesi di Trento, Trento (Archdiocese of Trento, Trento); FHL microfilm 1,388,952.,image

01794; "Italia, Trento, Diocesi di Trento, Registri Parrocchiali, 1548-1937," database with images,*FamilySearch* (https://familysearch.org/ark:/61903/1:1:XVYS-LP5 : accessed 5 January 2016), Alfonso Wegher in entry for Lodovica Candida Giulia Wegher, 15 Jul 1884, Baptism; citing p. 78, Santa Maria Addolorata, Sporminore, Trento, Italy, Archdiocesi di Trento, Trento (Archdiocese of Trento, Trento); FHL microfilm 1,388,952., image 01799; "Italia, Trento, Diocesi di Trento, Registri Parrocchiali, 1548-1937," database with images,*FamilySearch* (https://familysearch.org/ark:/61903/1:1:XVYS-GQ5 : accessed 5 January 2016), Alfonso Wegher in entry for Lodovica Giuseppa Maria Wegher, 09 Jan 1886, Baptism; citing p. 81, Santa Maria Addolorata, Sporminore, Trento, Italy, Archdiocesi di Trento, Trento (Archdiocese of Trento, Trento); FHL microfilm 1,388,952. image 01802

"Italia, Trento, Diocesi di Trento, Registri Parrocchiali, 1548-1937," database with images,*FamilySearch* (https://familysearch.org/ark:/61903/1:1:XVYS-P46 : accessed 5 January 2016), Alfonso Wegher in entry for Carolina Giuseppina Wegher, 10 Nov 1889, Baptism; citing p. 91, Santa Maria Addolorata, Sporminore, Trento, Italy, Archdiocesi di Trento, Trento (Archdiocese of

Trento, Trento); FHL microfilm 1,388,952.image 01812

McDonald, op. cit.

Bolognani, op. cit. p. 250

https://answers.yahoo.com/question/index?qid=200 90518160729AATe6F0, Yahoo Answers

Dickinson County, op. cit.

Ancestry.com. *Wisconsin, Birth Index, 1820-1907* [database on-line]. Provo, UT, USA: Ancestry.com Operations Inc, 2000. Edward J. Bonino, 17 Mar 1891, D001 Record 002073

Marcotte, Ruth, email sent Friday, May 21, 2010 1:58 PM, in possession of Wendy Negley

McDonald, op. cit.

Chiesa Cattolica, op. cit.item 22 image 1060.271

Family search, Wisconsin County, op. cit.

"Italia, Trento, Diocesi di Trento, Registri Parrocchiali, 1548-1937," database with images, *FamilySearch* (https://familysearch.org/ark:/61903/ 1:1:XVYS-DBM : accessed 22 January 2016), Luigi Giulio Wegher, 01 Apr 1860, Baptism; citing p. 10, Santa Maria Addolorata, Sporminore, Trento, Italy, Archdiocesi di Trento, Trento (Archdiocese of Trento, Trento); FHL microfilm 1,388,952. image 01729

Grave stone, Cemetery Sporminore

Marcotte, op. cit.

State of Wisconsin Marriage Certificate, copy in possession of Wendy Negley, original in possession of Marian Hampton. Also, Ancestry.com. *Wisconsin, Marriages, 1820-1907* [database on-line]. Provo, UT, USA: Ancestry.com Operations, Inc., 2000.

Original data: Wisconsin Department of Health and Family Services. *Wisconsin Vital Record Index, pre-1907*. Madison, WI, USA: Wisconsin Department of Health and Family Services Vital Records Division Marcotte, op. cit.

17 COMOX, BRITISH COLUMBIA, CANADA

Chapter 10:

The Move to Comox, BC and On

Meanwhile, far to the West, in 1864, rich veins of coal were found on Vancouver Island. Nothing was done on this discovery until 1888 when 8 mines were opened. The area was the Comox Peninsula with the mines being located in Courtenay and Cumberland. In 1891 the Comox Free Press opened. Between the newspaper and the mine company the call for miners was put out and many came. Frank Stefani was one of these.

He must have liked the physical environment as it is very beautiful and he could see mountains very much like the ones at home. On 12 Apr 1892 his first child, Frederic Frank Stefani, was born. Frank must have been very proud. He had a son! This was very important to men of that era.

However, mining coal was somewhat different than iron ore. The mines frequently filled up with toxic methane gas and there were many fires and explosions. Also, he had wanted to live in America. Thus, when news of mines in Washington State that were looking to hire miners came to Comox he must have decided to move again. He is listed in the King County Land Records Index as signing a contract with William H. Mercer on 29 May 1893 and is a grantee on a deed on 22 Jun 1893 in the town of Englewood. This town was renamed Gilman and eventually called Issaquah, which is how it is known today. In 1890 there were 200 voters in the town, population in 1900 was 700, so it was about the same size as Sporminore. And like Sporminore, it was at the foot of three mountains and in sight of two Mountain Ranges— the Cascades and the Olympics. Frank probably felt at home there.

His second son, John Frank Stefani, was born 27 Aug 1893. The Washington birth records list him as Steffen, John, mother, Tinetti Angelia, 22, father, Steffen, Frank 30, Miner,

Ausstra. Frank must have felt he was exactly where he wanted to be, with a wife, two sons and a job.

End notes Chapter 10

https://en.wikipedia.org/wiki/Comox,British_Columbia
Online publication - Provo, UT, USA: Ancestry.com Operations Inc, 2005.Original data - United States, Selective Service System. World War I Selective Service System Draft Registration Cards, 1917-1918. Washington, D.C.: National Archives and Records Administration

Wikipedia, Comox, op. cit.

Family Search, Washington County Land Records, King. Deed and Mortgage Index-indirect, 1876-1903, SN-SZ, image 164

https://en.wikipedia.org/wiki/Issaquah,_Washington
Online publication - Provo, UT, USA: Ancestry.com Operations Inc, 2010.Original data - Washington Births, 1891-1919. Various county birth registers. Microfilm. Washington State Archives, Olympia, Washington.Original data: Washington Births, 1891-1919. Various, image 232, p. 235

18 GILMAN (ISSAQUAH) WASHINGTON **1900**

Chapter 11:

Life in Issaquah, Washington

In the late 1890's the coal mines were starting to play out. Frank was able to buy five houses as people left the area. He initially rented them out, thus adding to his income. He became a saloon keeper, which in a mining and logging town was undoubtedly a profitable pursuit. The family lived in the back of the saloon.

On 7 Mar 1895, his daughter, Edith Rosetta Stefani, was born. She was soon followed by another daughter, Adelina Justina Stefani, on 29 Nov 1896. This was followed though, in February 1898, by the death of his son, John Frank, of whooping cough. By 1900 he had sold the saloon after a few incidents with violent drunks, one of whom left him wounded with a knife when he tried to interfere in a fight. He decided he didn't want to lead that kind of a life anymore. By now he was living in one of his five houses on Hill Street. The next child, Mary Victoria, was born here on 14 Mar 1900. She was followed on 29 Apr 1904 by a son, Francis Eugene George, who, sadly, died on 24 Jan 1908, of seizures. Finally, on 1 Mar 1908, another son was born, Clement Eugene Stefani.

19 EDITH, FRED, MARY, ADELINA (DEL),
ANGELINA, CLEMENT, FRANK STEFANI CA **1906**

One event that occurred around this time was that Frank left the Catholic Church. He had, of course, been raised in the Church. There was no other Church in Sporminore and the life of the town revolved around the Church, one was baptized, married and buried there as all one's ancestors had been for hundreds of years. When Frank came to America, he continued to be a faithful Catholic. But four key incidents changed that.

There was a Catholic Church in Issaquah, St. Joseph's. The services were held in the area starting in 1884 with a building built in 1896. The Church building was largely a result of three Irish residents of the town providing the land and materials. The priest was also Irish. The Irish had been the earlier immigrant group (coming in large numbers in the 1840's and 50's during the Irish potato famine). They were looked down on when they arrived and had persevered and established themselves as a group. Now, in their turn, they looked down on the Italians, the newest large immigrant group. Frank and family were categorized as Italian.

The first incident with this Irish priest had to do with Frank's oldest son, Fred. Fred came home from Sunday school crying because when he hadn't answered the catechism questions well enough the priest had given him a beating. Frank was not pleased with this. Around this time, the priest was drinking in Frank's saloon and was very derogatory about Italians. Again, Frank was not happy.

His daughter, Edith, tells a third incident, "A friend of my father's, who worked in the mines with him, was killed in the mines. The priest only came to our town one Sunday a month. Well, it wasn't his time to come so my father walked twelve miles to Renton, which was the next largest town, to get the Priest to come to have the ceremony for his friend. The Priest asked if he was a good parishioner and if he had given to the Church every Sunday. My Dad said he didn't know but he didn't think so. Therefore, the Priest didn't come. Thus, Dad quit going to the Church. We were all going to catechism every Sunday but all our friends were going to the Baptist Sunday School and Church. We wanted to go down there. We never could go because my folks were

Catholic. But when Dad didn't go to the Church any longer my folks said we could go to the Baptist Church but we had to go every Sunday, if we change, we had to go every Sunday. Well, we were delighted! We said we would and we did!"

Finally, the last straw was this incident as relayed by Frank's daughter, Adelina:

"[Frank] furnished the wine for the Catholic Church. The priest would come by Sunday morning to pick it up. Dad would get so tired working so late Saturday night cleaning up the saloon that he finally said, 'Father, I will give you the key and then when you need the wine, you can go in and help yourself.' The Father had to come from Renton to Issaquah for the mass so by the time he arrived he was tired.

"Well, Dad didn't know what he (the priest) was doing, he went in and was helping himself all right and by the time he would get to the Church he would be all kicked out of shape. The Church members blamed Dad for the priest getting woozy so they really turned Dad against the Church, because, as he said, 'If a priest can't maintain himself to be respectable to his Church and also drink up my profits, then I don't need his religion.' So, he left the Catholic Church and we went to the Baptist Church from then on."

Another incident Adelina shares regarding the saloon is this one:

"One night the Town Marshal came into the saloon and tried to calm down a drunk. The drunk was getting the best of the Marshall so Dad went to his assistance. The drunk had a knife and Dad got cut up terribly. Dad said after that, 'Whenever I see another fight, I'm looking the other way.'"

It was incidents like these that convinced Frank to get out of the saloon business. He worked for the railroad for $30 a day for a while. He sold the four houses he had and bought a laundry. This was a family venture. He had his son, Fred, manage the laundry. His daughters did the manual labor, washing and ironing. Frank, himself, drove the horse and buggy to pick up and deliver the laundry. They also hired some local girls to help with the manual labor. His daughters resented the fact that they were doing all the work while Fred was "managing." The laundry did not turn out to be a good investment, not enough money was made to pay the hired girls. So, Frank sold it along with the horse and buggy!

20 FRANK AND THE LAUNDRY BUGGY CA **1908**

At their house on Hill St. Edith remembers Frank having a big garden. "We had quite a large yard and Dad had the garden. He dug up the ground completely all around the house except the front of the house. Mama always had flowers in the front garden, but Dad always had a big garden, and the best in the city. He was always proud of it. We had a number of apple trees, a gravenstein, we had a Bartlett pear tree that was always loaded with pears and we had a plum tree. We also had currant bushes and gooseberry bushes. Dad always raised a pig and we had two cows." He also hunted and brought back fowl and even frogs' legs for them to eat.

21 FRANK, ANGELINA, AND CHILDREN ON THE PORCH OF THE HILL STREET HOUSE IN ISSAQUAH ABOUT 1910

Frank was remembered by his daughter-in-law, Peechie, as being very stern and with quite a temper. Edith tells it like this: "She (her mother) was always so thoughtful and kind to all of us, defended us from Dad when he came

96

home cross. Dad, every once in a while, would come home kind of tipsy and he'd go to the cupboard, have some cheese and bread and then he'd go to bed. So, we were always glad when he was tipsy because he was really good hearted then!"

At this point he went back to the coal mines and worked while saving up his money to buy a farm. This is what he had always wanted.

Family Search, Washington County Land Records, op. cit., 1907-1909, image 198, 295, 298, 303

Negley, Wendy, Transcript of interview with Peechie Stefani and Edith Kells 13 Jul 1979

Online publication - Provo, UT, USA: Ancestry.com Operations Inc, 2010.Original data - Social Security Administration. Social Security Death Index, Master File. Social Security Administration.Original data: Social Security Administration. Social Security Death Index

Online publication - Provo, UT, USA: Ancestry.com Operations Inc, 2010.Original data - Social Security Administration. Social Security Death Index, Master File. Social Security Administration.Original data: Social Security Administration. Social Security Death Index

Online publication - Provo, UT. USA: Ancestry.com Operations, Inc., 2012.Original data - Find A Grave. Find A Grave. http://www.findagrave.com/cgi-bin/fg.cgi: accessed 27 February 2012.Original data: Find A Grave. Find A Grave. http://www.findagrave.com/cg

Online publication - Provo, UT, USA: Ancestry.com Operations Inc, 2010.Original data - Social Security Administration. Social Security

Death Index, Master File. Social Security Administration.Original data: Social Security Administration. Social Security Death Index

Negley, Wendy, notes from conversation with Edith Stefani Kells, 1962; Gould, Virginia, Stefani Family Tree, data copied by Wendy Dec 1978

Online publication - Provo, UT, USA: Ancestry.com Operations Inc, 2008.Original data - Various county death registers. Microfilm. Washington State Archives, Olympia, Washington.Original data: Various county death registers. Microfilm. Washington State Archives;

Online publication - Provo, UT. USA: Ancestry.com Operations, Inc., 2012.Original data - Find A Grave. Find A Grave. http://www.findagrave.com/cgi-bin/fg.cgi: accessed 27 February 2012.Original data: Find A Grave. Find A Grave. http://www.findagrave.com/cg

Online publication - Provo, UT, USA: Ancestry.com Operations Inc, 2010.Original data - Washington Births, 1891-1919. Various county birth registers. Microfilm. Washington State Archives, Olympia, Washington.Original data: Washington Births, 1891-1919. Various, image 774

http://issaquahhistory.blogspot.com/2015/03/st-patricks-day-and-issaquahs-recent.html

Interview with Wendy Negley 16 Jan 2016

Transcript 17 Nov 1979, op. cit.

Gould, Virginia, op. cit.

Transcript 17 Nov 1979, op. cit.

22 STEFANI FAMILY **1918**

BOY ON LEFT: CLEMENT STEFANI

BACK ROW: ERIC EMANUEL, DOROTHY STEFAN, LUCAS KELLS,

MAXINE STEFAN, FRED STEFAN, ARTHUR STEFAN, FRANK STEFANI,

FRONT ROW: MARY EMANUEL, DEL ADAMS WITH HAROLD ADAMS,

EDITH KELLS WITH LYMAN KELLS, NELLIE STEFAN WITH VIRGINIA STEFAN,

ANGELINA STEFANI

Chapter 12:

A Farmer at Last

Sometime between 1900 and 1910 the family moved to a house on Hill Street. This is where they are listed in the 1910 and 1920 U.S. Censuses. In all three Censuses, 1900, 1910 and 1920, despite his various business ventures during these years, Frank's occupation is listed as "Miner." However, during these years he was always working toward his goal of owning his own farm. He is quite active in the King Co. Land Records in buying, selling and mortgaging various properties in and around Issaquah.

Meanwhile, his children were growing up. On 19 Jan 1912, his oldest son, Fred, married Nellie Elizabeth Brown. The family story is that Nellie didn't want to be married to someone with an Italian last name. So, Fred dropped the "i" from the end of his last name and became Fred Stefan. His sister, Edith, was quite unhappy about this as she thought it was upsetting to their dad. She stopped speaking to Fred and almost didn't attend his funeral many years later. She was, however, one of the witnesses on his marriage certificate so there may have been more to this falling out at a later time. Also, Frank himself is named "Steffen" on many of the early Issaquah records, so perhaps he also used this version of the name. Fred and Nellie's first child, Arthur Frederick, was born 10 Jan 1913 and three younger sisters were born one a year for the next three years. In 1916 two of Frank's daughters married: Adelina married John Adams on 22 Mar 1916 at the County Courthouse in Seattle with Edith again witnessing and Edith married Lucas C. Kells on 15 Aug 1916 in the family home. Two years later, Mary married Eric Emanuel on 30 Mar 1918 at Edith's home in Seattle. Interestingly, Fred was one of the witnesses to Mary's wedding and he signed his name as Fred Stefani, not Stefan. Adelina and Edith both had sons born in 1917 while Mary's daughter was born in September 1918. So, by January 1919, Frank and Angelina had 7 grandchildren.

In 1920, Frank finally managed to purchase and move into a farm. This was a poultry farm in the Issaquah Valley. It has been in the family ever since but is currently being sold. He raised on the average 5,000 chicks when he started with incubators in the basement and a separate brooder house to take the chicks to after birth. Peechie told this story of him in the early chicken hatchery days: "He used to have a whole bunch of brooders going and had a heck of a time, they'd pile up and die on him. Then one time his son-in-law talked him into putting in hot water heat for the chickens. They got this big long chicken house set up and put in the hot water system, and Grampa was sitting there. He was going to stay up and watch 'em and his son-in-law said, 'You can go to bed, that's all going to be taken care of. It's going to stay on the thermostat the same heat and nothing's going to happen to those chicks.' No one could tell him anything. He sat there in the chair and he stayed up and watched to make sure everything was alright! After that, things got a little bit easier for him."

He raised a big garden and worked hard. He used to clear the land and go out there and no matter how hard it rained he was out there. Eventually he discovered that it was more profitable to buy the already hatched baby chicks. He was raising as many as 10,000 or more. The eggs and chickens were sold to the Washington Co-op. He also kept cows, horses and pigs and tended fruit trees, nut trees, berry vines and grapes. Del recalled, "He always had a beautiful garden of vegetables, fruit, apples, etc." Which Clem said was "for family and livestock." He allowed Angelina to have a flower garden by the house, although according to Del, he always said, "But you can't eat flowers!"

In the 1930 and 1940 U.S. Censuses he is listed as a Farmer of a Poultry Farm!

End Notes Chapter 12

Year: 1910; Census Place: Issaquah, King, Washington; Roll: T624_1657; Page: 1A; Enumeration District: 37; Image: 669. US Federal Census 1910; Year: 1920; Census Place: Issaquah, King, Washington; Roll: T625_1924; Page: 1B; Enumeration District: 37; Image 1

Year: 1920; Census Place: Issaquah, King, Washington; Roll: T625_1924;

Page: 1B; Enumeration District: 37; Image 2

Online publication - Provo, UT, USA: Ancestry.com Operations, Inc., 2012.Original data - Washington State Archives. Olympia, Washington: Washington State Archives. Original data: Washington State Archives. Olympia, Washington: Washington State Archives. Image 41

Negley, story of…, op. cit.

See number 2 above

Online publication - Provo, UT, USA: Ancestry.com Operations Inc, 2010.Original data - Washington Births, 1891-1919. Various county birth registers. Microfilm. Washington State Archives, Olympia, Washington. Original data: Washington Births, 1891-1919. image 488

Negley,…Gould…op.cit.

Washington State Archives, op. cit.,image 484

Washington State Archives, op. cit., image 1268

Washington State Archives, op. cit., image 1074

Washington Births, op. cit., image 214

Washington Births, op. cit., image 161

Washington Births, op cit., image 310

Gould, op. cit.

Transcript 13 Jul1979, op. cit.

McDonald, op. cit.

Gould, op. cit.

Year: 1930; Census Place: Gilman, King, Washington; Roll: 2490; Page: 2B; Enumeration District: 285; Image: 143.0.

Year: 1940; Census Place: Gilman, King, Washington; Roll: T627_4344; Page: 1A; Enumeration District: 17-78 image 4

23 STEFANI FARM CA 1935

GRANDDAUGHTER MARGARET KELLS, ANGELINA, AND EDITH

Chapter 13:

Life on the Farm

Frank and Angelina worked hard (as usual!) and became successful poultry farmers. Their youngest son, Clement, got married on 21 Dec 1929 and moved into a house right next door. He married Pietje Bergsma, daughter of immigrants from the Netherlands. Her name is pronounced "peachy" and that's how she was known. She rapidly became one of the sisters! In the 1930 US Census Clem and Pietje are living right next door to Frank and Angelina. Frank is listed as a Poultry Farmer and Clem as a Farm Laborer.

By 1930 Fred had six children, two boys and four girls. Edith had four, two boys and two girls while Mary and Dell each had two (a girl and a boy for Mary, two boys for

Dell). Clem's two children came along in 1931 and 1940. So, by the end of 1940 there were 16 grandchildren! It was the custom for the family to gather on the farm every Sunday or so. In those days this was a long trip as there was no bridge over Lake Washington, from Seattle one had to drive around the lake. Fred, Edith, Mary, and Dell all lived in Seattle so they all drove that distance every week.

One of the grandchildren, Margaret Kells, wrote her memoirs of these visits and I am going to let her tell the story:

"My Kells family always thought of this drive to my grandparents' poultry farm in a fertile green valley near Issaquah as "Going up to Grandma's" because she was always there to hug and greet us when we arrived. Grandpa never showed up until dinner time in answer to the ringing of an old cow bell kept handy on the back porch. As we rounded the numerous curves of the Sunset Highway, we anticipated the final one beyond which we could see the green roof of the farm house.

"We turned off the paved highway onto a dirt road where a garage had a full-length sign on top reading

STEFANI POULTRY FARM. The car went past a field, a chicken house, a chicken yard with a stream flowing through, a storage house containing bales of straw, a small shed containing chicken feed, and then around a bend we passed another chicken yard, fruit trees, a pig sty, and last, an outhouse next to a tool and wood shed in the back yard of the house.

"Probably all of us enjoyed visiting the barn and tumbling in the hay even though Grandpa didn't like it so we kept it to a minimum. We also had fun climbing up on the bales of straw where it was stored but Grandpa discouraged this, too. (Poor Grandpa!) In season we helped pick some of the ripe fruit (cherries, prunes, apples, crab apples, pears, quince, blackberries, raspberries, loganberries, and purple grapes) to take home for Mother's canning and jelly or jam making. There were strawberries, too, but they all went for eating then and there.

"A sound I enjoyed hearing was the loud tick tock of the kitchen clock like those on the wall at school. It chimed on the hour and half-hour. The large crank-up wall telephone was of interest, too. It was a multi-party line so not all rings were to be answered. Sometimes Grandma would quietly listen in to another's call which we children were discouraged from doing as well.

"When needed, our family went up to Grandma's on a Saturday to help get ready for a holiday dinner next day. I especially liked to watch the process of preparing the chickens from live bird to roasted meat. First Grandpa would take them one by one from the cages in which he had previously put the poorest egg layers. Then he would chop their heads in turn on the big chopping stump nearby. This looked rather gruesome because they would squalk loudly in alarm, struggle to get away, and run around headless for a few minutes before falling over. When the task was completed, Grandpa would carry them by their feet so the blood would run out as he walked back to the house.

"Next came dipping them into scalding hot water (oh, the smell of wet feathers!) to loosen the feathers, the plucking onto newspapers spread on the dining table (what a mess!), the singeing of hairs over the kerosene stove burner, the cutting open and cleaning out (another messy job!). After washing each they [were] stored in a cool place.

"The major holidays were the best times at Grandma's. The dining table was always heavily laden with food, featuring roast chicken stuffed with her rich dressing. Each family had brought part of the food for dinner and supper so the preparation for up to 30 people could be shared. Grownups sat together in the kitchen at the big table while children sat at card tables in the living room. There was always much good-natured talk and laughter to listen to especially from the kitchen.

"The chickens and farm animals were always in evidence. Grandpa had six double hen houses with fenced yards. He didn't like for us to go inside to disturb the chickens so we watched them running around and pecking outdoors.

"I liked better to watch Grandpa milk the cows in the barn stalls and to see him fill their eating places with hay and a grain mixture. They chewed away with obvious satisfaction while yielding their milk at the other end. Sometimes work horses grazed in the pasture and accepted the bunches of grass we tossed over the fence. Occasionally a pig or two was being fattened in the pig sty for later butchering by Grandpa.

"There were semi-wild cats living in the barn who appeared at the house only at feeding times. We knew that kittens had been born only when their mothers led them up to the house with them. They never ventured close enough for petting or being held.

"The collie dogs played the multi-role of farm helper to bring in the laggard cows, watch dogs, and pets to follow Grandpa around or lie under the dining table at his feet ready to accept food scraps if offered. They ate from metal containers filled with leftovers by Grandma and set on the back porch. Much of their sleeping was done behind the warm kitchen range where Grandma complained of the smell of wet fur being dried out.

"When it was time to go home in the early evening, we always told Grandpa good-bye but Grandma always gave each a big hug first.

"Life on the farm was obviously hard work but both grandparents assured the family that their valley land was God's country in which they were happy to stay."

End notes Chapter 13

Washington State Archives, op. cit. image 1454

1930 Census, op. cit.

McDonald, Memories…, op. cit.

24 FRANK STEFANI AGE 82, 1945

Chapter 14:

Retirement

In the 1940 Census Frank is again listed as a Farmer of a Poultry Farm. He is 76 years old. The value of his home is listed as $2,000. He worked 48 weeks the past year and the past week he worked 84 hours! Frank finally retired in 1945 at the age of 82. However, he kept active on the farm. At the age of 85 he cut 400 fence posts and piled them!

His granddaughter, Margaret Kells, writing about her memories of Frank and the farm has this to say about him:

"When I think of my grandfather, I see him first sitting at the end of his oval-shaped kitchen table either eating a sizeable meal or puffing on his corncob pipe afterwards. He seldom said much to contribute to the family conversation unless aroused to get into an argument. Such political subjects as President Roosevelt's New Deal, Social Security and Welfare programs were sure to get him talking in heated terms. He expected men to do for themselves rather than being "lazy bums" dependent upon government handouts. His children heard that "The hand that is all take should be cut off," which was straight from the Old Country of Austria.

"Since he had worked hard all his life for what he had, he felt that others could and should too. As a poor immigrant to America in his youth he had worked at running a saloon in Canada[sic], at being a coal miner in Issaquah, WA, a landlord of several rental homes that he had acquired at the same time, and finally a poultry farmer. To supplement his food supplies for a large family, he planted fruit and nut trees, grew berries, grapes and vegetable gardens, hunted and fished, scoured the fields for edible plants and creatures. The children did not necessarily like the food that he found (such as frogs, mushrooms, watercress) but they tried to eat some of it anyway rather than go hungry.

"Grandpa enjoyed playing cards (poker, rummy, pinochle) or cribbage at the dining table with Grandma or family members at night after chores were done. He was a shrewd, methodical player who often won while slapping his cards down with finality. His pleasure at winning was accented by sounds of satisfaction. Beating uncle[sic] Fred was a major accomplishment because he was the best opponent.

"On my occasional overnight stays, I can see him at the sink pouring himself a small glass of homemade wine for a nightcap. His wine also appeared at our family gathering dinners for the adults. My parents did not care much about drinking it and one taste for me was enough for me ever.

"There were several rifles on the wall rack over Grandpa's bed which he took down whenever hawks, skunks or wild cats tried to get at the chickens. He was a good shot because we would find the evidence sometimes when we came to the farm next day. The skunks could hardly be missed!

"Outdoors I can see my grandfather trudging between chicken houses with his collie dog at his side. When my grandfather went to milk the cows in the barn, I sometimes followed him there. It was interesting to watch him fill the stalls at the head end with forkfuls of hay plus canfuls of a powder mix. Then he let the bawling cows in to crowd into their stalls to begin feeding while he milked them one at a time. He perched on his 3-legged stool and if a cat came near, he squirted some milk into its mouth. He usually had 2 or 3 cows to tend.

"Several times when there was a new calf to be weaned, my grandfather would dip his righthand middle finger into a bucket of milk, put it into the calf's mouth to suck and them lead it down to the bucket for it to continue there. The calf got the idea easily. What a great trick!

"My grandfather had obvious Old-World ideas that affected me when it came to my efforts to lose weight as a teenager. He insisted that I looked just right from the Italian standpoint where they liked strong, healthy women able to work hard. When it came to women's-work he expected them to labor in the field and garden as well as the home. That meant that Grandma kept the family vegetable garden tended between household chores but also helped out when larger jobs needed workers. When the hay was ready for gathering and rain storms were predicted before long, Grandpa called on the larger family, including women, to come help.

"For a special occasion such as a wedding or funeral my grandpa could be prevailed upon to get dressed up in a suit and tie to attend along with Grandma. To me he looked strangely out of place. Since he always had to get back to milk the cows on time, he could never stay as long as Grandma would like. At least he did make the effort to be part of these ceremonies as much as he could."

In another place Margaret writes, "[Frank's] most notable character traits were rugged individualism, strict honesty, persistence, ambition, self-sacrifice, unyielding principles, stern discipline and hard work."

End notes Chapter 14

1940 US Census, op. cit.

Gould, Remniscing…, op.cit.

McDonald, Memories…, op. cit.

25 FRANK AND ANGELINA 50TH WEDDING ANNIVERSARY
FRED, EDITH, MARY, DEL, AND CLEM STAND BEHIND.
2 JUN **1941**, ISSAQUAH, WASHINGTON

Chapter 15:
Fifty Years of Marriage

In 1941, Frank and Angelina celebrated their fiftieth wedding anniversary. They were married on 2 June 1891 thus the fiftieth was 2 June 1941. In 1941, though, June 2nd was on a Monday so, they held the celebration on Sunday, June First.

This was a big deal. Not everyone lived long enough to celebrate fifty years together. Marian remembers that all her aunts were excited about it and about what to wear. They all looked for lace dresses and made sure that they were different colors but that the colors didn't clash! Marian's Dad, Clement, and her Uncle Fred, wore suits. They posed for a family portrait and indeed, Angelina has on a long lace dress and her daughters are each wearing a just-below-the-knee length lace dress. Frank and his sons are wearing suits and ties. The women each have a corsage on their left shoulder and the men have a boutonniere. Angelina is wearing small drop earrings, her girls each have earrings right up against the ear. Angelina, Mary and Dell each wear a brooch in the center of the neckline, while Edith has none. I see no other jewelry, no necklaces, bracelets, watches but one can see Angelina's ring. All dressed up for the occasion!

The event was well attended by friends and family who came from all over. All the family came. Angelina was pleased because many older friends came and all the neighbors attended as well. Marian says that, "Everyone who was still breathing came!"

There were two cakes which had been specially made and purchased in Seattle for the occasion. One was for everyone to eat. The other one was for display and admiration! It was shaped like a big open book. On the page on the left was the date and place that they were married, on the right was the date and place of their anniversary. We can assume that it said 50 in big frosting numbers!

We can imagine that Angelina must have been happy to see her friends and family and thought back over the years. Did she remember the young girl from Torre Canavese and the hopes and dreams she brought to America with her? Were there thoughts of Canavese in her mind?

End notes Chapter 15

Negley, Wendy, notes on phone conversation with
Marian Hampton

26 CANAVESE, TORRE BAIRO, AND TORRE CANAVESE

Chapter 16:

Canavese

Canavese is a valley at the foot of the Alps in Northern Italy, a "subalpine geographical and historical area in Province Torino". It is in the region of Piemonte or Piedmont in English. The name, Canavese, means "village at the foot of the mountains" and it was originally the name of a political and commercial district called Canava or Canaba north of Turin. This was a trade center and marketplace for the foodstuffs grown in the region.

Writing in 1363, Peter Canavese Azario describes the area as follows, (translated from the Italian) "Dotted with hamlets, villages and castles of wooded mountains, it boasts scenic areas rich with crops, vines, lawns and especially waterways. There are animals in large numbers and deposits of iron in the mountainous areas in the Alps . . ." Canavese could be described in the same way today.

The first peoples known to live in the area were the Salassi, a tribe of Cisalpine Celts. "Cisalpine" was the Roman designation meaning "this side of the alps (the Roman or Italian side!)" Lucan, a Roman writing at the end of the First Century BCE, portrayed the Salassi as fierce warriors having long auburn colored hair. They had gold mines in the southern part of their territory which the Romans took from them. The Romans founded a city there called Eporedia, present day Ivrea. The Roman Legions defeated the Salassi in a battle in 25 BCE, killing or enslaving most of them. Many were already living in Ivrea, though and they remained. The Salassi, as a tribe, disappear from history at that point, but chances are that their descendants remain in the people in the area today.

After the Fall of the Roman Empire, Canavese was run by the Byzantine Empire. It was an area frequently invaded and taken over by different regimes. In 568 the Lombards invaded and took it over from the Byzantines. In

722, the Franks under Charlemagne invaded and captured it. By 1051 the Counts of Canavese ruled. In the 14th Century it came under the House of Savoy. In the 15th Century it went under the Spanish then the French, then back to Savoy, finally Napoleon added it to France until 1815 when the House of Savoy took it back. The Castello Ducale in Aglie (near where Angelina lived) was originally built by a Count of San Martino under the Count of Canavese and taken over by the Duke of Savoy. Eventually the head of the House of Savoy became the King of Italy when it was united in 1861, putting Canavese solidly in Italy.

There is quite a bit of French influence in Canavese and the Piedmont Region. In fact, it has its own dialect called Piedmontese which owes a great deal to French. The word for Canavese in French is Canavais and in Piedmontese it is Canaveis.

Canavese is a fertile valley and agriculture is very important. The main products there are rice, wine, maize (corn), potatoes and white truffles. There are also many fruit trees and vegetables grown.

Per Visits Italy.com, "The Piedmontese as a whole, Torinese in particular, have perennially exhibited a feistiness of spirit and an independence of mind." (So perhaps the Salassi, who fiercely resisted Roman rule, have not disappeared after all!)

End notes Chapter 16

https://en.wikipedia.org/wiki/Canavese
http://www.corsac.org/serra.html

corsac, op. cit.

corsac, op. cit.

https://en.wikipedia.org/wiki/List_of_Celtic_tribes
https://en.wikipedia.org/wiki/Ligures

https://en.wikipedia.org/wiki/Salassi

Wikipedia, Canavese, op, cit.
https://en.wikipedia.org/wiki/Piedmontese_languag
e; Wikipedia, Canavese, op. cit.
http://www.italyworldclub.com/piemonte/
http://www.visitsitaly.com/italy/piedmont/turin/tur
in/index.html

27 VIA GIACOMO TINETTI IN SAN MARTINO CANAVESE

Chapter 17:
The Tinetti Family

The name Tinetti is quite unusual. It is only found in Piemonte (except there are one or two people with that name in Lombardy which is the next region over). In the present day there are 31 families of that name in the Province of Torino, most in a few towns in a small area right where Angelina came from. There is no one of that name in her home town today, though. The name seems to be from a nickname. "Tino" is frequently used as a nickname for such names as Martino or as "Alberto" which becomes "Albertino" and then "Tino." Probably meaning little or just an affectionate ending. Tino also means vat or tub in Italian and may be an occupational name for someone who made or used vats. Then "etti" is added meaning little, "tino" "etti" or Tinetti. It is often found in records as "Tinetto" as well.

This is because in Italian the singular for a name is "-o", Tinetto, and the plural is "Tinetti". The Tinetto version is even rarer than Tinetti.

Angelina was born in the town of Torre Canavese but her father and grandfather weren't. Her grandfather was born in San Martino Canavese, which is right next door, and, in that town, there are a great many Tinettis! The family traces back to Pietro Tinetti who baptized a son in San Martino on 2 Feb 1676. One can assume that he was born about 1650 but a birth record for him has not been found in San Martino records. It could be that he was born in another town but that has not been established. We can justifiably call San Martino our family's home town! There even is a Tinetti Street there, named after Giacomo Tinetti who is not on our direct line but I'm sure is related.

One of Pietro's great grandsons was Martino Tinetti. He was born 28 Feb 1745 in San Martino, son of Pietro Tinetti. He married Giovanna Antonia Maria Amosso. Their marriage record is not in the San Martino records, which means that she was from another town and they were married there. Marriages usually took place in the bride's parish. Martino and Giovanna had a large family of fourteen children of which Guiseppe Tinetti was the tenth.

28 PARISH BIRTH RECORD OF GUISEPPE TINETTI
(HERE NAMED JOSEPH AS IT IS IN LATIN)
4 JUL 1784 IN SAN MARTINO

He was born 4 Jul 1784 in San Martino. He married Maria Magdalena Pastore on 11 Feb 1805. He was Angelina's grandfather. Giuseppe and Maria moved to the nearby town of San Giovanni where they had eight children. There is a family story that he was a chef for the Grimaldi's of Monaco and returned to Italy at the time of Garibaldi (1848-1861). This has still not been verified. However, he does disappear from the records at the right time span. This research is still being done!

Historically, Monaco was a Protectorate of the Kingdom of Sardinia from 1815 to 1860. The Kingdom of

Sardinia included Sardinia, Savoy, Piedmont and Genoa and was ruled by the House of Savoy. Piedmont was the region that initiated the movement to unify Italy starting in 1848 and at the culmination of that in 1860, Monaco became an independent Principality, Savoy and Nice went to France and Piedmont, Genoa, and Sardinia became part of Italy. But from 1815 to 1860 Monaco was essentially part of the same country as Canavese, so it is quite possible that Guiseppe lived and worked there.

His son, Giovanni Battista Tinetti, was born on 14 Jul 1825 in San Giovanni, Torino. He was Angelina's father. What is his story?

End notes Chapter 17

http://www.gens.info/italia/it/turismo-viaggi-e-tradizioni-italia?cognome=TINETTI#.VpbgmPkrKM8

http://italia.indettaglio.it/eng/cognomi/cognomi_piemonte.html

http://www.ganino.com/cognomi_italiani_t

Chiesa Cattolica, San Martino Canavese, Piemonte, Battesimi 1590-1899, FHL Microfilm, 1603623

Photo of street sign in author's possession

Chiesa, op. cit.

Chiesa, op. cit.

Chiesa, op. cit.

Gould, Virginia, attributed to Bill Burr, in a note which author has a copy of

http://monacodc.org/monhistory.html

Data copied from "souls parish register" in Torre Canavese parish church, copy in author's possession

29 PHOTOGRAPH OF GIOVANNI TINETTI TAKEN ON **28** JUN **1897**
AND USED ON CARD TO COMMEMORATE HIM.
IT WAS SENT TO ANGELINA AFTER HIS DEATH IN **1904.**

30 BACK OF CARD SENT TO ANGELINA IN **1904**
IN MEMORY OF HER FATHER
IT READS "MRS. FRANK STEFANI, IN MEMORY OF YOUR FATHER,
TINETTI GIOVANNI,
BORN IN JULY **1825**, DIED **11** OCTOBER **1904**".

146

Chapter 18:
Giovanni Tinetti

Giovanni (John) Tinetti was born on 14 July 1825 in San Giovanni, a *frazioni* (or hamlet) of Castellamonte. This is a town near San Martino where his parents, Guiseppe (Joseph) Tinetti and Maria Pastore were born and married. He may have spent some of his childhood in Monaco where his father perhaps worked for the prince as a chef. Otherwise, he was raised in San Giovanni where he was living when he married Domenica Zanotti-Cussio of Cuceglio (another town in the same area). Domenica and Giovanni were married on 27 May 1846 in Cuceglio according to family data or on 27 August 1846 in San Giovanni where the marriage is recorded. Her sister, Cattarina, was a witness. The official noted that Domenica was illiterate and couldn't sign her name but made her mark and that Giovanni's father,

Giuseppe, was also illiterate. Giovanni signed his name, however.

While still living in San Giovanni, Giovanni and Domenica had two sons: Guiseppe Ottavio, born 20 Nov 1846 and Antonio Amedeo Secondo, born 30 Mar 1849. Between Antonio's birth and the birth of their daughter Maria Teresa on 19 July 1853, they moved to the town of Torre Canavese and specifically to the *frazioni* of Valia. Valia consists of one road and a few houses on a hill just past Torre Canavese. They lived in a three-story house with a marble staircase and large rooms. There are balconies on the second and third floor. On each side of the house were cattle stalls and in the back of the house was a spice mill where Giovanni ground and packaged spices for a living. The records all use the term "contadino," which means peasant or farmer, for his profession. There also was a garden for growing the spices and other vegetables for the family. A large cherry tree also stood in the back (and still grows there). A few yards to one side of the house was a lake as well.

31 THE GIOVANNI TINETTI HOUSE AS IT WAS FOUND IN 2014.
A TINETTI COUSIN IS IN FRONT.

32 THE CHERRY TREE BEHIND THE TINETTI HOUSE

The next child, Maria Teresa Emilia (later nicknamed Gin) was born on 24 March 1855. She was followed by a stillborn child on 1 February 1858, Virginia, born on 27 July 1859 and another stillborn child born 12 January 1862. The two stillborn children undoubtedly affected Domenica emotionally and physically. She died on 2 April 1863, cause of death not shown on the death certificate.

This left Giovanni with five young children ranging in age from 16 to 3 ½. To help him cope, Domenica's younger sister, Catterina, came to look after the children. After a while, Giovanni began to feel that it wasn't seemly for her to be living there with him and no supervision. So, he told Catterina that he would marry her in name only to protect her reputation. According to family lore, she replied, "Giovanni, I will gladly marry you but only in a full and true marriage." And so, they were married. [8]

---

[8] Catterina was born Maria Catterina Zanotti-Cussio on 26 Jan 1830, daughter of Secondo Zanotti and Teresa Cussio (as was Domenica). Zanotti is also often found as Zanotto in the singular/plural

It is not exactly clear when Giovanni and Catterina began their union but on 22 January 1866 their first son, Giuseppe Secondo (named for both grandfathers!), was born. Unfortunately, he died only a few months later on 7 August 1866. Happily, he was soon followed by twins. Maria Teresa Domenica and Maria Teresa Rosa who were born 15 October 1868 in Valia. Domenica became known as Minnie and the other twin was called Rosa. Less than two years later, on 14 June 1870, Maria Teresa Albina (known as Albina) was born. For some reason the Maria Teresa naming pattern was dropped after that point for on 4 September 1871, Angela Margherita was born but on 4 May 1877 Adele Seconda Maria Teresa was born so the Maria Teresa pattern returned. Note that Angela was called by the more affectionate version of her name, Angelina, and likely, Adele was called Adelina.

---

form similar to Tinetti. "Zan" is an old form of John so it basically means "little John,"the "-otti" ending can also mean "younger" so it may just be "Johnson!" Cussio is also a very rare name from the Cuneo area near Canavese. It seems to be from the name Cussa, found on a memorial stone from Roman times, "CVSSAE."

In 1868 the oldest daughter, Maria Teresa married a Tinetti cousin, Giuseppe, who died in Jan 1872. The same month she remarried, Giovanni Preto. Her sister, Maria Teresa Emilia "Gin," married in 1877. So, growing up Angelina would have been living with two much older brothers, four older sisters and one younger sister. [9]

Sometime around 1883 Giovanni's son, Antonio, got into some financial difficulty. (It was either Antonio or one of Giovanni's brothers, the data is unclear). Giovanni had to sell all his properties to make good on a bill incurred by his son. He had been a well-off man and now he was poor. This resulted in several of his children leaving for America. In 1884 his oldest son, Giuseppe, arrived in America on 5 October.

---

[9] Her younger sister, Adelina, died on 27 Dec 1880 at the age of three years. Angelina was nine years old. In January 1881, her half-brother, Antonio, was married. On 25 Mar 1881, her older sister, Maria Teresa, died at age 29. On 7 Feb 1883 Virginia died at age 23. By the age of 12, Angelina had lost three sisters!

Exactly what happened to Giuseppe is unclear. He is found on a passenger list arriving in New York on 5 Oct 1884. According to the family records he died in the San Francisco earthquake and fire in April 1906. His name has been found in the records of the victims of the quake. He may have had a family as there are Tinettis who turn up in Northern California after 1906. More research needs to be done on this.

Meanwhile, on 16 Aug 1885, Rosa married Luigi (Louis) Bonino and they left for America. Minnie went with them or followed soon after for we find her marrying Pietro Giovanni (Peter John) Peretti on 20 Jun 1888 in Coal City, Illinois. This left Albina and Angelina at home with their parents.

Rosa and Luigi left Illinois and went to Hurley, Wisconsin where they ran a saloon to cater to the miners in the booming coal and iron mining industries. In 1889, they sent for Angelina to join them and work for them in the saloon. Why Angelina and not Albina is not clear, Albina may have been married by then or soon to be or she just didn't want to leave home! Luigi paid Angelina's fare and she was to repay him by working in the bar which she started to do as soon as she arrived. [10] Here she met a young miner, Frank Stefani. They were married on 2 Jun 1891 in Hurley. She wore a lavender dress with a fur collar. Her parents are named in the Marriage Certificate as John Tinetti and Katrina Zenota and her birthplace as Sues, Italy. Louis Bonino witnessed the marriage. Frank had to finish paying off her fare to America to Luigi after which they moved to Canada.

This left Giovanni and Catterina at home with Albina, although she may well have been married by this time. She married Marchello Bonatto and they had four children, they were married by 1900 when their daughter, Domenica was born.

Angelina most likely had a good childhood. She and her three sisters were close. The area around the house was a

---

[10] Frank Stefani was working as a miner and was in partnership in another saloon and stopped in at Luigi's one night. He saw Angelina and told his partner, "I'm going to marry that girl"!

nice one in which to play, there was the lake and the cherry tree. No wars took place right in their neighborhood. Her father was well off enough that they didn't go hungry or always have to worry about food. Her parents were loving to each other and the children as far as can be told. Certainly, she never complained to her own children about her childhood She and her sisters remained close. She wrote to and visited with her sisters Rosa and Minnie and they visited her. Albina wrote to all three. Albina and Maria Teresa Emilia ("Gin") were close in Italy, both living for a while in Torre Bairo, and their grandchildren are still friends.

Giovanni died on 11 Oct 1904. Someone sent Angelina a photo of him taken 28 Jun 1897 in Torino giving his birth and death dates. The exact place of death is unknown. Catterina's death information is yet to be found. Giovanni, through his two wives, had nine children who lived to adulthood, at least 30 grandchildren with uncounted

great-grandchildren and generations beyond. Would

Angelina be able to say the same?[11] [12] [13]

---

[11] This is the family story. In researching the records, I am unable to find a record of their marriage until 14 Aug 1878. This is after their last child was born! Perhaps the earlier record had been lost and they did a new one to ensure all was legal. Maybe they didn't get around to it until then. However, none of the children's birth records say that they are illegitimate. Perhaps they were married somewhere other than Torre or Cuceglio Canavese. It's just speculation but the only record found so far is for 14 Aug 1878!

[12] "-ina" is an affectionate ending added to girls' names. Angelina was actually christened Angela but was called Angelina all of her life. Adele would have been called Adelina. Angelina named one of her daughters Adelina after this little sister.

[13] This is the Stefani version of how Frank and Angelina met. The Bonino family version is in Frank's story. The Bonino version has the feel of truth to me and I wonder if Frank ever told Angelina that story?

End notes Chapter 18

Chiesa Cattolica, Parrocchia di Sporminore (Trento), Salt Lake City, Utah: Filmato dalla Genealogical society of Utah, 1986. Film/DGS 1568341, San Giovanni (Baptisms, Marriages and Deaths, 1576-1923) marriage of Giovanni and Domenica is 827.194 Chiesa Cattolica 1568341 op. cit.

Chiesa Cattolica op.cit. 1518380 Torre Canavese Chiesa Cattolica 1518380 op.cit. 80.951, 113.858, 104.452

Chiesa Cattolica op.cit. 151382 Cuceglio familyeducation.com

Chiesa Cattolica op.cit. 1518380 Torre Canavese Chiesa Cattolica op. cit.

New York, Passenger Lists, 1820-1957 Year: 1884; Arrival: New York, New York; Microfilm Serial: M237, 1820-1897; Microfilm Roll: Roll 481; Line: 27; List Number: 1282

Chiesa Cattolica op. cit. Matrimonia 1866-1900 image 117

Ancestry.com, Illinois, County Marriage Records, 1800-1940

Ancestry.com, Wisconsin Marriages 1820-1907, marriage certificate owned by Marian Hampton family, Issaquah, Washington

Letter from Marco Coltro, 2014, in possession of the author

Card shown at beginning of this chapter, owned by Marian Hampton family, Issaquah, Washington

Chaplin COTTAGE GALLERY.

33 ANGELINA (STANDING)
ROSA AND LOUIS BONINO WITH
ANGELINA AND PEARL, THEIR TWO OLDEST DAUGHTERS
ABOUT **1890** IN HURLEY, WISCONSIN

160

Chapter 19:
Angelina

We have already seen how Frank and Angelina moved first to British Columbia and then to Issaquah. Angelina was having babies and taking care of them, the house, and Frank. She seemed content to follow him in these moves and indeed the family's fortunes improved with each. But there was one time that she refused. Around 1900, Frank went to Alaska during one of the Gold Rushes that occurred in the last decade of the 19th Century and the first decade of the 20th. He didn't find gold but he was very, very impressed with the size of the produce grown in Alaska. They had a short growing season but grew very big fruits and vegetables. He told her that he wanted to move up there and own a farm. She told him no. She wouldn't go. No way. Immovable. So, he gave up that idea!

Angelina was a midwife, a quite well known active one. One imagines that she supplemented her household budget that way. In his eulogy the Rev. Wm. Hanson said of her, "In these past 56 years, Angelina Stefani has been mother not only to her own 7 children, but to uncountable men and women whom she has brought into the world, as comfort and helper of many, many young mothers. Whenever someone needed to be sat up with at night, whenever advice on the curing of a croupy cough or a prolonged thumb sucking, whenever anyone needed help or experienced assistance, Angelina Stefani was always ready to go. Mrs. Stefani extended her family beyond those whose name was Stefani."

Angelina always supported Frank. When he left the Catholic-Church she left with him. When he started a laundry, she helped run it. When he bought a chicken farm, she incubated eggs and raised chicks. When he had a faithful dog, she put the scraps out for the dog. They were, indeed, partners. He was the head of the family, though.

One ruling he made was that she was not to speak Italian. He said they were Americans now and they would only speak American. How she felt about this is not recorded. However, her granddaughter Marian Stefani tells this story. Marian's mother, Peechie (in Dutch, Pietje), was Dutch and her family often spoke Dutch among themselves so Marian had heard the Dutch language being spoken. In Issaquah there were many Finnish immigrants and she had also heard that language. but she had never heard her Stefani grandparents speak Italian (since they didn't speak it anymore). One day when Frank was out working on the farm, an Italian woman came by selling some sort of baked goods. Angelina happily spoke Italian with her. Marian hearing this ran home to her mother and excitedly said, "Mama, Mama, Grandma's speaking Finnish!" Peechie was quite amused and explained that she was speaking Italian. Presumably they saw no reason to mention it to Frank!

Angelina had her own strong viewpoints. One person she didn't much like was her daughter-in-law, Nellie. Perhaps it was because Fred changed his last name (from

Stefani to Stefan) in order to marry her. Or perhaps she felt Nellie looked down on her as an immigrant, Nellie was from an old American family. Or just a personality clash. Or the not uncommon difficulty that a woman has with the woman who marries her first-born son. Who knows? But Angelina didn't like her and was quite critical of her to other family members but not to her. One day at a family gathering on Sunday, Fred and Nellie's daughter, Maxine, crawled under the dining table. While she was there unnoticed, Angelina started to talk about Maxine's mother in a very derogatory manner. When Maxine went home, she told her mother all about it. As a result, Nellie never came to the Stefani home again. Fred still came and brought the children but Nellie stayed at home. One can imagine what she may have said to her husband about his mother and what he might have said to his mother! But that rift was never repaired.

On the other side of the ledger, however, Frank and Angelina took in one of Fred and Nellie's children and practically raised her. By 1924, Nellie had six children including a new baby. This was a bit much for her. So, Frank and Angelina took the fourth child, Virginia, who would have been about 8 years old and had her live with them. They were a big influence on her and years later she researched the family and made the only (until now) family history book of the family. Much of her material was used in the research and writing of this book.

Angelina, apparently, didn't really like to cook. So having the family over every Sunday and all holidays was a strain on her in that area. The girls all brought various parts of the meal but it was her daughter-in-law, Peechie, who did most of the cooking, helped by her daughter, Marian. This way Angelina could enjoy seeing her children and, especially, her grandchildren. She had an excellent relationship with Peechie, also an immigrant, having been born in The Netherlands.

Angelina took care of the children and the house. She sewed all of the girls' clothes and every year she canned 50 jars of blackberries!

Angelina kept in touch with her sisters, Rosa and Minnie, and their children. For instance, the Issaquah Press ran this article on 8 Sep 1911, "Fred Stefani and his mother and brother, Clement, his cousin, Mrs. Angeline Flor [Rosa's daughter] and son left yesterday morning for a visit with friends in Illinois and Oklahoma. Mrs. Flor is returning to her home in the latter state, while Fred and his mother will be gone about six weeks." Rosa lived in Oklahoma and Minnie lived in Illinois. The family has pictures of several children and grandchildren of Minnie and Rosa visiting their cousins in Washington State over the years.

End notes Chapter 19

Transcript of 14 Jul 2001family interview p. 12
Hanson, op. cit.

Negley, notes on interview with Marian Hampton

Washington Archives, op. cit. nwskgmc02796,
image 41
Negley, op. cit.
Negley, op. cit.
Negley, op. cit.
Transcript of interview with Edith Kells 17 Nov
1979
Issaquah Times, 8 Sep 1911

34 FRANK, ANGELINA,
THEIR SON, CLEM,
AND GRANDDAUGHTER, MARIAN,
IN MAR 1942

Chapter 20
A Portrait of Angelina by Her Granddaughter

Angelina's granddaughter, Margaret Edith Kells, wrote the following portrait of her:

"My Grandmother played the central role for us visiting grandchildren so we always thought in terms of "Going up to Grandma's" rather than "Grampa's". It was only as an adult that I learned how Grandma had carried over to America from Italy the matriarchal role for women. Examples:

"1. Each time we grandchildren arrived for a visit or left to go home, she would give us each a big hug and kiss whether we wanted it or not, especially the boys. Each of our mothers was loaded down with food to take home and the room was filled with fond goodbys.

"2. She took the lead in the kitchen work while the daughters surrounded her to help. Hers were the major parts of the dinner and supper while the rest brought their contributions to it.

"3. She wrote quite often to her daughters telling them when the fruits were ripe for picking, when help was needed in house or field, when chicken houses needed cleaning, or making plans for holidays and other visits. I liked to read her letters because she learned to write English according to the sound of words which did not account for the silent letters. Conversely, she pronounced words according to the letters they contained. Therefore, her written words left some letters out (an for and) and her spoken words put them in (k-nee, k-nock). When we made fun of this, Mother would explain how she had learned the hard way without benefit of school.

"4. Since Grandma didn't like for children to appear on the farm wearing impractical clothes, we girls had better not wear our Sunday dresses and slippers. She also thought that girls should keep their legs covered so we had to wear long or knee socks rather than anklets when they came into style. These rules came through Mother, however.

"5. Grandma expected everyone there for holidays which sometimes caused friction in our own family because several times there was our high school championship football game or we needed to sing in the choir. Only once was mother prevailed upon to let Lyman attend the game and take the bus up later. Grandma showed so much displeasure to Mother that she vowed never to let it happen again.

"6. Grandma went to all weddings and funerals in the family if she had a way to get there. Sometimes she came by bus to spend part of the day especially when we were little. She also came to help her daughters when the children were born. When Mother was desperate for medication after we twins were born, my father resisted giving her a drug. However, grandma slipped it to her anyway because she knew how much it would help.

"7. If it had been my grandma's decision neither I nor Doris would have gone to the University because, "Why does a girl need to go when she is just sure to get married and have children?" My Dad insisted on higher education for all his children, however, even though my mother felt that Business College had been plenty good enough for her.

"8. Even though Grandpa was responsible for earning and dispensing the money, Grandma collected and spent that which came from door sales of chickens, eggs and butter. Instead of always telling Grandpa when the collection bowl was full, she hid bills in the linen closet for later use. It was that money which bought us a refrigerator and large items for others in the family. This was kept secret from Grandpa to prevent arguments and give Grandma some leeway.

"9. Both grandparents favored the traditional first-born son. This lucky one was Uncle Fred who was also born first. Imagine the joy of his parents! Through the years Uncle Fred fostered resentment in the other children because they were expected to help him succeed despite their own preferences. When he was just starting out in the laundry business, his sisters had to do the hard work without pay while he was handling the service end. They never forgot how unfair this was. Uncle Fred visited the farm much less frequently and did less to help than the others but yet his folks were happier to see him and his family when he did show up. This was a bone of contention all through the years, also.

"10. Grandma kept in touch with relatives in the U.S. and Italy too. She was always happy to have nephews visit her when they were passing through from other places. During World War 2 she responded to family letters appealing for food and clothing by collecting as much as possible from family and neighbors to send to them. "They think everyone in America is rich!" she would complain. [1]

"11. There were maxims from Italy that Grandma taught her daughters and which I heard from my mother. Consider these:

When her children wanted something that they could not have, Grandma would tap her cheeks exclaiming, "Go up in the sky and get it!"

About loose talk she would say, "Talk is cheap but it takes money to buy whiskey!"

About doing a complete job sweeping the floor she would direct, "Don't sweep only where the Pope walks!"

About bearing troubles she would counsel, "Everyone has his own sack of rocks to carry!"

"12. Grandma willingly cared for other people's children when she saw the need. My Cousin Virginia lived on the farm during early childhood because Aunt Nellie (Uncle Fred's wife) could not manage one more little-one at that time when she already had three. Later she was to have six all together so Grandma practically raised Virginia. Grandma also cared for any children that the hired men brought along. [2]

"13. Both Grandparents were too proud and independent to ask for help outside the family unless they absolutely had to and could pay for it or return the favor later. Some relatives and others found this hard to accept when they wanted so much just to do a good deed for them.

"Addition: When it came to health matters, Grandma still relied upon herb and nature remedies. Every spring she gathered bark from the barberry tree from which she brewed a bitter liquid which acted as a strong laxative. Her children had all had its benefits but we grandchildren had all been tricked one at a time to take a spoonful. We each rushed to wash out our mouths with water amid loud protestations. Never again!

"Some pictures that linger in my mind about Grandma are these:

"Mixing large amounts of bread dough at a time— arms plunged into a wash tub full. How good the loaves smelled when baking and how appetizing when lined up on the sideboard!

"Churning milk at the kitchen table to get butter which took a long time. Working out the whey to consolidate

175

the butter also took a long time. Forming the bricks and applying the design came last.

"Quietly listening to the party line when the number of the telephone rings were not Grandma's own. We children were not allowed to do the same, however.

"Slapping her playing cards down in irritation when she was losing. This abruptly ended the game on a sour note.

"Carrying out the chamber pots in the morning to empty in the outhouse. Later after the bathroom was installed that chore ended. Soon Grandma had a sturdy shelf put over the tub so she could have a cool place for cottage cheese making and other uses. I sometimes wondered if the tub ever got used for baths!

"Scraping up all the left-overs to make full pans of dog and cat food which went on the side porch for eating.

"Life on the farm was obviously hard work but both grandparents assured us that their valley land was God's country in which they were happy to stay. Their influence on their family lives was strong, a mix of the Old World and the

New. I am sure not to be the only one with many happy memories."

[1] Marco Coltro, grandson of Angelina's sister, Albina, told me that much of what was sent did not reach them and what did seemed odd to them, not really what they needed. She sent coffee which was good but the wrong kind of rice, cigarettes which they didn't need and gum which he didn't use! Albina was living in Torre Bairo at the time of World War 2. She took the grandchildren and fled to the mountains for safety. She gave the food that could be found to the children and died of malnutrition in 1944.

[2] As an example, the 1940 Census lists the hired man, Charles Kirby, and his daughter, Virginia, age 14, as living on the farm with Frank and Angelina.

End Notes Chapter 20

McDonald, memories of Stefani Grandparents,
op. cit.

35 MARGARET (GRANDDAUGHTER), ANGELINA, AND EDITH

1935, STEFANI FARM

Chapter 21:

Letters From Angelina

In 1945, Frank retired from the farm. He sold his stock and ceased operation. His son, Clement became concerned about Frank and Angelina living by themselves on the farm. He persuaded Frank and Angelina to move in with him and his family. The two houses were next door, separated by a creek with a footbridge. Angelina didn't want to move. However, little by little they began moving their things to the new house. One day while on the footbridge carrying things to her son's house, Angelina had a heart attack. She went into the hospital and was there for a number of weeks, her daughters visiting daily. Finally, on 10 June 1947 she died. Her memorial service was held on 14 June 1947.

Frank moved in with Clement. He died 19 Nov 1953 with a Memorial Service on 21 Nov 1953. They are buried together in Hillside Cemetery in Issaquah with their two young sons and Clement and Peechie at their sides.

Two letters that Angelina wrote seem to belong here. The first was written to her grandsons, Lyman and Milton Kells on 14 May 1945. In part it reads: (all spelling and punctuation is as she wrote it)

"By the way some news we are going to get new linolium in the ketcking and a new ketching stowe as sone as we can get them we got new curtains yesterday I tougt I tell you so you wont fall over when you see it. I hope it will be soon dear boys pray that they leave you come back to see your father and mother the Joy to them and you too, and Grampa and myself don't know how long i'll be here I am really low down, well I am getting shor of paper I say goodby to both of you from all of us for ever/ Grandpa and Grandma Stefani."

And this to her granddaughter, Margaret and her husband, John, written on 4 Mar 1947, only three months before she died:

"Dearest granddauther and grandson

"I received your surprising letter from Chicago I could not thinking wo was writing to us from there as I dind recognize your end writeing unti I read it and was very glad to hear from both of you. and what please us more is to hear that you and Jack are very happy and try to fello Granpa's foot steps of his young days wen we was like two birds just flying out of mother's nest but Grandpa allway work faytfully at anything onest and always try to save a little but wat he got he neva made it by the bushuls, at that time the wages was small 2.00 a day of 10 hours was good pay and with good manegment we allway save a little evrething was chipper then and we never take in sports or anything that take our money that he sweet so ard to get and we were glad by our lonosom together like your mother & father ave been in ther life together and rasing their family at the best of their ability.

God bless them with grand hope that all of you will succide like we did or better, there is better chances now.

"Now I send you both our best regards & hope that this will find you all well like it leave us.

"For ever you grandma and grandpa Stefani

"let us hear about you always"

Finally in her granddaughter Marian's autograph book she wrote,

"January 1st 1940

"Remember me hearly remember me late me at night when you go to bed

"Your loving Grand Mother

"Stefani"

We remember.

End Notes Chapter 21

Hampton phone interview, op. cit.

Transcript of interview with Peechie Stefani et. sl. 14 July 2001

Washington, Select Death Certificates, 1907-1960, Ancestry.com. 2014 Ref no 87 100, FHL film 2032616

Hanson, op. cit.

Washington, Select Death Certificates, 1907-1960, Ancestry.com 2014, Ref ID 20247, FHL film 203321

Reid, op. cit.

Stefani, Angelina letter 14 May 1945, in author's possession

Stefani, Angelina, letter 4 Mar 1947, in author's possession

Stefani, Angelina, entry in Marian Hampton's autograph book in Marian's possession

36 FRANK STEFANI

Chapter 22:

Frank's Last Days

A house, beloved and familiar though it may be, can be very lonely after your spouse of 56 years has died. Frank Stefani found himself more and more spending time at the house next door, the house of his youngest son, Clement, and his family. At first it was just for meals and passing an evening. Finally, he asked his son to move his bed from his farmhouse and let him move in. He was given the back bedroom on the first floor where he could look out on the garden, stream and woods.

According to his granddaughter, Marian, his coming changed the rhythm of the household. He awakened early and expected his usual breakfast of oatmeal, pancakes and eggs. When Marian and her brother just grabbed juice and toast before school he would call out, disapprovingly, "An empty sack never stands" as they ran for the school bus.

Frank was a man who had always worked hard with physical labor. He continued this even in his retirement. He was almost 84 when Angelina died. At the age of 85 he cut 400 fence posts a day and was very proud of it—even the Minister mentioned this feat in his eulogy. He set about clearing the land of stumps and blackberry vines between Clem's house and Tibbets Creek. The first years he slowly, methodically, dug, chopped and burned the brush. One large stump had had the center burned out so he turned it into a makeshift shelter for himself. He could be seen sitting on a box, smoking his pipe and surveying his accomplishments for the day in this cozy spot. As the land became more cleared, and he got older, he gradually moved with more effort and sat to work from a wooden box that he inched along. His dog, Rusty, stayed close by.

At last, a garden emerged where onions, garlic, and tomatoes were grown to be added to the dandelion greens for the salads he loved. Often, he reminded his family not to let the blackberry vines take back over the yard again after he was gone. They said they wouldn't but never really thought he would be gone.

Then one day the old yellow cat didn't come home and they knew he was gone for good. Frank spent more time napping on the couch and telling stories of his early life. He spoke of his love for this country and urged his grandchildren to vote and pay attention to politics to keep the country strong. He felt the Puget Sound area was God's country, as he told his granddaughter, Margaret. He told his granddaughter, Marian, that the Issaquah Valley was the most beautiful spot in the world.

Frank loved his adopted country. When Social Security came in, his wife, Angelina, said they should apply as they had paid taxes for many years. He said, "This country doesn't owe me a thing, Mama, nothing, I owe this country lots." He let her apply and when the allotments came, she used hers for household expenses but he never cashed his. After she died, he sent his all back.

Eventually, as he approached the age of 90, his legs gave out and he became unable to walk. Peechie described it, "He was working all the time. And then finally his health kind of broke. His legs just didn't seem to want to carry him anymore." He said, 'I get up in the morning and I want to get up and get the fires going and work out there.' And he said, 'I'd get up and, you know, my legs wouldn't carry me, I'd have to go back to bed. Oh, my,' he continued, 'that was the hardest thing I ever had to go through. I couldn't get out and work.' And then one day, he fell. He was pushing a chair in front of him cause his legs wouldn't hardly hold him and he was trying so hard to get around. He slipped and fell and he never walked after that. He stayed in bed and his daughters came and took care of him. He was in bed about, I'd say, about a little over 10 months. But he was fine, he didn't have any pain. It was just that his legs wouldn't pack him around. He played pinochle in bed with Clem and argued politics to me. He was never in pain or sick or anything. He just slipped away, old age, his heart kind of gave out. But he had a good life. He seemed real happy. He lived to be 90 years old and three months.

"He was getting close to his 90th birthday and I said, 'Boy, do you know you're going to be 90 pretty soon?' And he said, 'By golly, that'd be pretty wonderful to live to be 90 years old.' And after he got to be 90 well, then he thought that was a good life he had and he sort of just went downhill. We had Open House for him and My! He thought that was the most wonderful day."

He was very unhappy being bedridden. His old dog, Rusty, dug a bed for himself right outside of Frank's window and spent his days lying there until Rusty died, curled up in his flower bed nest below Franks bedroom window. They buried him where the old stump had been.

Clement built a birdhouse outside of Frank's window so he could watch the birds build a nest and hatch their young. He enjoyed watching this but said that he could see that women rule. With the birds, if the Mama bird didn't like a twig, the Papa bird had to find another one. So, it is with people. He had thought he was in charge but he could see that really his wife ruled the house. Peechie adds, "And he says, 'I tell you the birds are like the people, just raising the devil down there!' But they finally got the nest made and he watched them raise the young ones and watched them fly and he had the window open so he could see everything. He was pretty good natured when he was sick. He never got cross or nothing."

His daughters came and visited regularly, taking turns caring for him so it wasn't just left to Peechie, his daughter-in-law. The family still came regularly on the weekend to visit and be together, as it had always done. But he just gradually succumbed, finally dying on Thursday, 19 November 1953 at 10:35 A.M. at the age of 90 years and three months. His funeral was held that Saturday, 21 November 1953(7).

After he was gone, his family was cleaning out his room. In his dresser in a drawer under his handkerchiefs they found a handkerchief with the embroidered initials MW as well as a photograph of Monica Remondini, his sweetheart to whom he had been engaged before he came to America. He never forgot her. Perhaps he thought of her sometime in his last few hours.

At his Memorial Service, the Minister, Rev. William L. Reid, said:

"Death comes stealthily into our gardens and steals away our flowers, but it cannot take away the power and presence that grew them. So, they grow again!

"Death comes into our homes and takes away our loved one, but it can only take away that which is mortal. It must keep its hands forever from all that which is eternal."

So, Frank, the blackberry vines have not been allowed to overtake the garden and your descendants have not forgotten you. We wish to know more about the place you came from and the ancestors who preceded you and us in this life. This book is for you and all your family, past, present and future, for the Stefanis of the Pale Mountains, the *Val di Non*, and Sporminore.

Endnotes Chapter 22

"Frank Stefani" handwritten account of Frank Stefani's last days by Marian Stefani Hampton, written about 1994, copy in possession of Wendy Negley, San Francisco, CA (all info used in this Chapter is from this source unless otherwise noted)

"Memorial Service for Frank John Stefani, Saturday, November 21, 1953" William L. Reid, R.D., Minister of the Issaquah Community Church, typewritten copy in possession of Wendy Negley

"Memories of Stefani Grandparents" by Margaret McDonald, written ca 1990, copy in possession of Wendy Negley

Op. cit. Hampton, p. 2

"Reminiscing with Aunt Dell (Adelina Stefani Dorner)" , transcript of an interview by Virginia Gould, no date ca 1970, copy in possession of Wendy Negley

Phone interview with Marion Hampton by Wendy Negley, 1 Mar 2015, notes in possession of Wendy Negley

Transcript of interview with Peechie Stefani and Marian Hampton13 Jul 1979

Op. cit. Reid, p. 1

Phone interview, op. cit.

Op. cit. Reid, p. 2

37 Monica remondini

Chapter 23
Final Words

Around 1950 when his granddaughters Marian and Virginia were cleaning, they found something of Frank's. Marian tells it like this:

"I remember that he had a handkerchief made of really beautiful linen with pretty handwork all around the edges of it and a name was worked into this lace. It had taken a long time to make it, and it was really pretty and the name was Monica. And when we asked him about it, (he had kept it way down somewhere and when we were cleaning his drawers, we found it, Virginia Kirby and I) we asked about it and we found out that this was the handkerchief that his girlfriend had given him when he had left wherever, Italy or

Germany or wherever he had left. And he was supposed to come back and get her and bring her to the United States when he had enough money. But, in the meantime, he had seen Grandma in the window of the tavern and fell in love with her while she was working as a barmaid someplace in Wisconsin. So, Monica, we never knew what happened to Monica and her handkerchief was still around!"

Frank left Sporminore, and Monica, in 1886 and built a life for himself and his family in America. Still, sixty-seven years later when he died, he had Monica's handkerchief and her photo in his room.

38 Cousin Marco Coltro, Torino (Turin) May 2014

AFTERWORD:
RETURN TO ITALY

In 2013, my sister, Rhonda Peterson, decided that she wanted to see the places our great-grandparents came from and wanted me to join her. So, we planned our trip. She did all the travel arrangements and I found family.

The information I had from Virginia's papers was that there was a grandson of Albina's (Angelina's older sister), named Marco Coltro, living in Turin in the 1980's who some family members had visited. No one knew where he was now, though. So, I found the Italian White Pages (Pagine Bianche) and found only one Marco Coltro in Turin. I wrote him a letter in English and used Google Translate to translate it into Italian. I included my email address and a diagram showing my descent from Giovanni Tinetti and his. I mailed this off and waited. I didn't hear and then one day I was deleting spam in my e-mail and saw "Cugini d'America". It was an email from him in my spam! He was happy to hear from me and to show us Torre Canavese when we came.

For Sporminore, I had no leads on cousins so I took a shotgun approach. Using the White Pages again, I entered "Stefani" and Sporminore and found five addresses of Stefanis living in Sporminore. So, I wrote to each one in Italian. I did the same for Wegher (Frank's mother's name) and Friedle (Frank's sister's husband's name). There were 3 Weghers and 2 Friedles. I heard from two Stefanis and one Friedle (now spelled Fridle), no Weghers. The Fridle was a great grandson of Frank's sister, Adelaide. We communicated via his daughter who speaks English. I sent him the picture we have of Adelaide. He hadn't seen it before. I discovered that the postcard we have from Sporminore was from his grandfather, Guido. He arranged to meet us in Trent and take us to Sporminore.

Ferrucio Stefani sent me a copy of his family tree and I was able to find our connection. We are 7th Cousins once removed! The other Stefani is Mario Agostini whose mother is a Stefani. He told me that he didn't have a family tree but

I told him I did because his mother is Ferruccio's cousin.

Both Ferruccio and Mario agreed to meet us in Sporminore.

So, we were all set with relatives to meet in Italy!

39 TORINO

AFTERWORD 2

Torre Canavese

Rhonda and I arrived in Torino on May 20, 2014. We met Marco and his beautiful wife, Maria Teresa Reineri. They took us to several places in Torino including the Duomo, the Chapel of the Shroud of Turin, the Royal Palace with its incredible Royal Library and the main walking and shopping street. Marco took us to two churches on hillsides, very beautiful inside, and from one of them he showed us the Canavese valley. It was very green with two rivers running through it.

On 22 May they took us to Torre Canavese. We met Italo Testa and his wife, Denise. He is the great grandson of Maria Teresa Emilia Tinetti, Angelina's half-sister. They showed us Torre Canavese, Cuceglio, San Martino, and San Giovanni, all very close together. In San Martino we saw WW I and II Memorials to Tinettis and a street named Tinetti for our cousin, Giacomo Tinetti (Plate 26). We toured the Churches in each town. Each one was a work of art inside: incredibly beautiful painted walls and ceilings, each different. The towns were neat, very clean and seemed prosperous. Marco said that most people don't live by farming there but work in Torino or other local towns. Italo works for Olivetti in the nearby city of Ivrea.

Finally, we went to Valia where Giovanni and his family lived. This is really just one road and 2 or three farms off of it. At the end of the road is the house where they lived. The Tinetti house was sold by Giovanni when he had to help his son, Antonio, out of some financial jam. The current owner has built new farm buildings and a house right across from the original house. The Tinetti house looked just as it does in the photos we have from 30 years ago, likely not much different than it looked when Angelina lived there. We went around to the back where we saw the beautiful view of the valley and the mountains beyond. A cherry tree grew there which Marco said had been there when Angelina lived there. We picked and ate cherries just as Angelina would've done 150 years ago. We also saw the lake by the house which has trout in it.

Italo and Denise were warm and welcoming and showed us great hospitality. Marco and Maria Teresa were incredible, giving us more than two days of their time and sharing their home with us. Both served us delicious meals of Torinese specialties. Angelina, Rosa, and Minnie would've been happy to find the family still there and flourishing!

40 Fridle family with Vittorio in the middle between Wendy and Rhonda in the Sporminore church 2014

AFTERWORD 3

Sporminore

Vittorio Fridle, great grandson of Frank's sister Adelaide, with his wife, Daniela, her sister and brother-in-law Giovanni, met us in Trento on May 23, 2014. Giovanni speaks English and lived in America for a while, so he was our interpreter. We drove to Sporminore, about a twenty-minute drive. We drove through Mezzolombardo where Giovanni Luigi Stefani, Frank's father, was raised by his mother and step-father. It was only about five minutes from Sporminore. We turned off the highway and went up a steep and somewhat windy road to enter Sporminore. It looked almost exactly like the 1915 postcard we have, except for the modern street signs and the cars. It was a town on a hill with the Church prominent in the middle and the mountains behind. When we drove up to the square there was a group of people waiting for us. These were our Fridle cousins, about 20 descendants of Adelaide all here to meet us and visit

Sporminore with us. Most didn't speak English although some did. Only a couple lived in Sporminore.

We first went to the Church and toured it. It was also beautiful inside with painted walls and ceiling. But it was darker, more ornate than the Churches in Torino, with a Northern, Austrian influence. This is the newer Church but it is the one that Frank would've known and worshipped at. He was baptized here. We took family pictures in front of the altar.

Next, we went to City Hall where we met the mayor. He also has Stefani blood and we concluded we are cousins. He presented us with three books (each), two on Sporminore and one about a priest from Sporminore who did Missionary work in South America. That one is called "Dio e coca" ("God and Cocaine"!). The mayor asked if we were members of *Trentino del Mondi* and we said we were which made him happy.

We then went to the school and sat at a long table and showed each other pictures of our families. Vittorio gave me a copy of their family tree. I showed them what I had done on the family on my tablet. We all shared photos of family and, of course, everyone loved the pictures of my grandchildren, Crispin and Elinor! After that we went to the cemetery which was in the yard of the old Church down the hill from the new one. We saw the Fridle family graves and found Monica Remondini's grave with her photo. It is common practice in Italy to put a photo on the gravestone. There was a memorial to World War 1 and 2 dead and Stefani, Wegher, Remondini and Melchiori names were on it, all descendants of family members.

We had lunch at the *Al Maso Ristorante* in Maso Milano. I told them that Frank and Adelaide's mother was born in Maso Milano which they didn't know. For lunch we had red wine, anti-pasta (three kinds of meat, pickles and local cheese), a dish with chunks of meat in a sauce, mushrooms, fried cheese, and a big ball made of bread and bits of sausage all mooshed together into a ball. These were all local specialties which Frank probably would've eaten. They were all delicious!

We went back to our hotel and rested until 5:00 when Valerio Rigotti and his daughter, Valentina, picked us up. He is also a great grandson of Adelaide and a 5th Cousin. They took us to see the Castle Spor (or, in Austrian, Spaur) which is a ruin near the town. It mainly is a tower on a hill which has been restored somewhat so that you can climb to the top and get a fantastic valley view. You can see three castles and many towns spread over the whole valley (*Val di Non*). I thought of Frank and Giovanni travelling to those towns to peddle their wares, a lot of walking! I'm sure that Frank had stood and looked at that view but perhaps he was thinking about what lay beyond this valley.

We then joined the whole family for dinner. We again went to Maso Milano but now we went further inland to a restaurant called *Baita* or mountain hut. It was decorated like a hunting lodge with deer heads on the wall.

We had the special Trentino "patate" which is a potato pancake. They are as big around as a dinner plate and 1-2" thick. It was delicious, sort of a cross between latke and hash browns. We had anti-pasto, a local vegetable that looked like spinach but was reddish-brown, with plank smoked trout, sauerkraut, and bread. And wine, water and caffe! Varelio said how much they enjoyed having us and invited us back soon. I told Giovanni to tell them how grateful we were for the hospitality they showed us. It was an "ahh" moment with the women putting their hands on their hearts and tears in their eyes. Rhonda and I felt that Frank would've been happy to see the descendants of his sister and know they were doing well.

The next day Rhonda and I walked around Sporminore in the morning to get a feel for the town. We ran into a woman named Rina who knew who we were. She was the widow of Mauricio Stefani and showed me the letter I had sent! She was Ferrucio's mother and Mario's aunt. She spoke no English but we were able to communicate with her quite well. She fed us lunch and introduced us to people who dropped in. Her grandson Alessandro has red hair just like my Cousin Larry's so now we know which side of the family that comes from! It shows the Celtic influence still lives here. We met Ferruccio briefly as well.

Then we met Mario and his mother. They took us to meet his great uncle, Ettore Stefani. He lives next door to Rina in a little house that has been in the Stefani family for no one knows how many generations. Ettore was one of 12 children who all grew up there. He was beaming and happy to see us. We discovered that Mario's mother had two sisters and that the three sisters call each other on the phone every day. Our grandmother, Edith, daughter of Frank, called her two sisters on the phone every day also! Stefani sisters—generations and miles apart but so similar!

In our walking around we found house 54 which was the house Frank's grandfather and father were born in and his mother died in as noted in the records. His birth record didn't give a house number but one would guess it would be the same. Sporminore also looked clean and prosperous with many new houses.

The next day Mario's father drove us to the train station in Trento. We said good-bye to Sporminore. It was such a thrill to be there and see it in person, meet the people who live there now and the relatives and connect the Old World and the New, like completing a circle. Great Grampa, this one was for you!

Fridle Family Descendancy Chart

Federico Fridle
nato a Haeselgehr (A) il 25/10/1858
a 1 mese si trasferisce a Trento e viene allevato da Luigi Zadra (calzolaio di Tres)
Nel 1885 va a SPORMINORE
Nel 1887 sposa Adelaide Stefani (muore di parto nel 1899)
Rimasto vedovo si risposa con Fortunata Oscari

Carmelio (1916-1986) + Irma Cristan (1923-2007)

Vittorio (1918-1943)

Vittorio (1946) + Daniela Bonato (1950)

Gemma (1949) + Mario Franchi

Tiziana (1953) + Doriano Finotti

Arianna (1974) + Luca Carli (1969)

Matteo Franchi + Simona

Martina Franchi

Alessandra + Fabrizio Mantovan

Sara Finotti + Stefano

Francesco Carli (1999)

Violante Franchi

Alice Franchi

Giulia Mantovan

Giacomo Mantovan

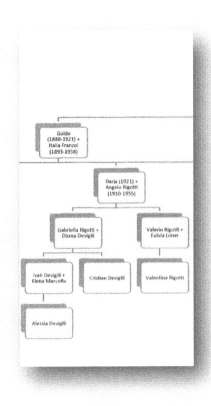

Famiglia Fridle

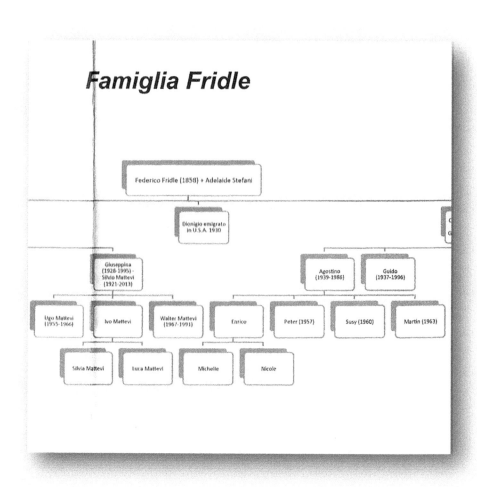

218

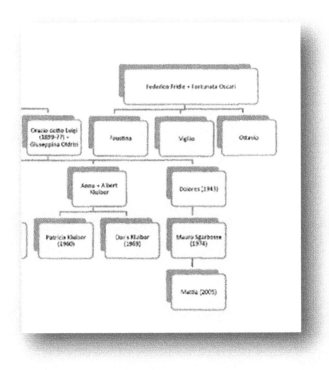

219

41 Monica remondini

AFTERWORD 4

Monica

One of the last things we did in Sporminore was to revisit Monica Remondini's grave. I wanted to be sure I had a photo of it and her photo on it. The custom in Italy is to remove the remains after 30 years and use the space to bury someone else. You must pay to keep your loved one in their grave beyond the 30 years. Monica died in 1931 so the family must have paid twice to keep her there. This speaks to how she must have been loved by her children and grandchildren. She and Frank both made their choice of how they would live their lives. I'm sure he would have been happy to know that hers bore fruit as did his. I felt that Frank would've wanted us to pay our respects to her and bring greetings from America. Another circle closed.

53 SILVER STREET IN HURLEY, WISCONSIN, 2022

BRIDGE AT LEFT WHERE FRANK CROSSED TO GO TO THE SALOON

AFTERWORD 5

Michigan

In May 2022, Bill and I visited the towns of Iron Mountain, Michigan and Hurley, Wisconsin. I was unable to find any addresses for Frank or for Rosa and Louis. In Iron Mountain the old railroad station from 1891 had been restored and was now the town museum. Unfortunately, they were in the process of further renovating and I was unable to do any research. It is probable that Frank and Angelina caught a train to Canada from this station though so it was good to stand on the platform and feel much as they did (It is no longer a working railroad station.)

In trying to find a possible location for Rosa and Louis' saloon I found that Hurley had a street, called Silver St. which was known for its saloons and houses of prostitution. That seemed like a possible area to look at. We put "Silver St" in the GPS and found ourselves crossing a bridge over a small river (I would have called it a creek actually). On the other side was Silver St. I realized that this was the bridge that Frank had crossed to get to the saloon. It was only about 6-8 feet long. I had imagined it as much bigger. It would have been easy for Frank to just walk across in the evening to go to the saloon. Looking at the line of buildings that were saloons and such only one had a window at street level that Frank could have looked in and seen Angelina. That was the first building as you came off the Bridge. I felt that that was the saloon that Rosa and Louis owned, in which Angelina had worked. The story I had heard many times was now real!

On the marriage certificate Frank was said to live in Pence. I looked this up and it is a town directly south of Hurley. The post on Google mentioned that one could still see cabins built by the "Italian" immigrant miners in the style they were used to from home. These were not in any particular spot but could be spotted in alleys or as you drove through. Bill and I drove around Pence and we did, indeed, spot some of these cabins. They were log cabins looking like mountain huts. The "Italian" miners were men from

Trentino (from the Tyrol) and the style they built in was of the mountain huts. I don't know if Frank lived in one of these but he would have been familiar with them.

57 CABIN IN PENCE BUILT BY MINERS FROM THE TYROL

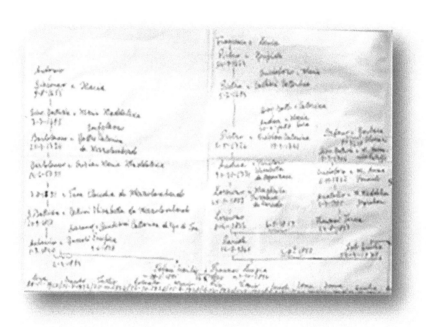

44 Ferrucio Stefani Family Tree,
the common ancestor is
Bartolomeo and Bottes, Caterina

226

STEFANI FAMILY RECORD
USING THE NGSQ SYSTEM

(The "NGSQ" System is the numbering system (*National Genealogical Society Quarterly*) published by the *National Genealogical Society* for recording family trees. The NGSQ System assigns a number to every child, whether or not that child is known to have progeny.

```
          (-Generation One-)
1 Progenitor
  +  2      i   Child
     3     ii   Child (no progeny)
     4    iii   Child (no progeny)
  +  5     iv   Child
          (-Generation Two-)
2 Child
     6      i   Grandchild (no progeny)
     7     ii   Grandchild (no progeny)
5 Child
  +  8      i   Grandchild
          (-Generation Three-)
8 Grandchild
  +  9      i   Great-grandchild
    10     ii   Great-grandchild (no progeny)
  + 11    iii   Great-grandchild
  + 12     iv   Great-grandchild
```

Unless otherwise indicated, all data here is from FHL Microfilm 1388952 Registri ecclesiastici di Sporminore (Trento), author: Chiesa Cattolica, Parrochia di Sporminore (Trento). The original microfilm has no image numbers, where I have viewed it online at *Family Search* or at the

227

Portland Family History Center, I have noted the image numbers. This is the data I was able to discover, I do not guarantee that the family groups are complete. I have taken it down to my grandparents' generation with much of my mother's generation. My own family I have done through my children and grandchildren, others I have not because I don't have all the data. With living people, I have only included names. The Sporminore records are records of baptism, in later records (after 1800) they did note birth and baptism dates but usually these are the same day. Where a separate baptism date is given, I have noted it, otherwise whatever date is given is noted as "b."

Abbreviations used:

abt. about,

b. birth,

bp. baptized,

d. death,

d/o daughter of,

d.s.p. (decessit sine prole) died without issue,

d.y. died young,

m. marriage,

n.f.r. no further record,

s/o son of,

unk. unknown,

unm. unmarried.

+ indicates the person whose line will be followed.

Genealogy Table of Contents

The Stefani Family   239

The Wegher Family   261

The Remondini Family   265

Remondini ancestors of Monica Remondini   268

Families Allied with the Remondini Family

    The Olmar Family   269

    The Franchetti Family   271

    The Melchiori Family   273

    The Magnani Family   274

    The Conci Family   276

    The Facchini Family   277

Descendants of Adelaide Maria Anna Stefani

and Federico Friedl   278

The Tinetti Family   282

Descendants of Maria Teresa Emilia Tinetti   290

Descendants of Maria Teresa Rosa Tinetti

and Luigi Bonino   292

Descendants of Maria Teresa Domenica

  "Minnie" Tinetti and Peter Peretti   297

Descendants of Maria Teresa Albina Tinetti

  and Carlo Marchello Bonatto   312

The Pastore Family of San Martino   313

The Motto Family   315

The Zanotti Family   315

The Bezutti Family   319

The Pastore Family of Cuceglio   319

The Cussio Family   320

The Henrico/Enrico Family   322

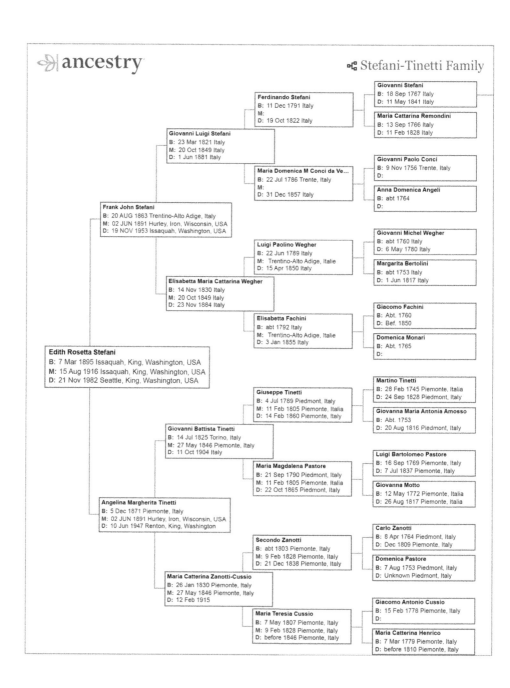

Giovanni Stefani
B: 18 Sep 1767 Italy
D: 11 May 1841 Italy

Maria Cattarina Remondini
B: 13 Sep 1766 Italy
D: 11 Feb 1828 Italy

Ferdinando Stefani
B: 11 Dec 1791 Italy
M:
D: 19 Oct 1822 Italy

Giovanni Luigi Stefani
B: 23 Mar 1821 Italy
M: 20 Oct 1849 Italy
D: 1 Jun 1881 Italy

Giovanni Paolo Conci
B: 9 Nov 1756 Trente, Italy
D:

Maria Domenica M Conci da Ve...
B: 22 Jul 1786 Trente, Italy
M:
D: 31 Dec 1857 Italy

Anna Domenica Angeli
B: abt 1764
D:

Frank John Stefani
B: 20 AUG 1863 Trentino-Alto Adige, Italy
M: 02 JUN 1891 Hurley, Iron, Wisconsin, USA
D: 19 NOV 1953 Issaquah, Washington, USA

Giovanni Michel Wegher
B: abt 1760 Italy
D: 6 May 1780 Italy

Luigi Paolino Wegher
B: 22 Jun 1789 Italy
M: Trentino-Alto Adige, Italie
D: 15 Apr 1850 Italy

Margarita Bertolini
B: abt 1753 Italy
D: 1 Jun 1817 Italy

Elisabetta Maria Cattarina Wegher
B: 14 Nov 1830 Italy
M: 20 Oct 1849 Italy
D: 23 Nov 1884 Italy

Giacomo Fachini
B: Abt. 1760
D: Bef. 1850

Elisabetta Fachini
B: abt 1792 Italy
M: Trentino-Alto Adige, Italie
D: 3 Jan 1855 Italy

Domenica Monari
B: Abt. 1765
D:

Edith Rosetta Stefani
B: 7 Mar 1895 Issaquah, King, Washington, USA
M: 15 Aug 1916 Issaquah, King, Washington, USA
D: 21 Nov 1982 Seattle, King, Washington, USA

Martino Tinetti
B: 28 Feb 1745 Piemonte, Italia
D: 24 Sep 1828 Piedmont, Italy

Giuseppe Tinetti
B: 4 Jul 1789 Piedmont, Italy
M: 11 Feb 1805 Piemonte, Italia
D: 14 Feb 1860 Piemonte, Italy

Giovanna Maria Antonia Amosso
B: Abt. 1753
D: 20 Aug 1816 Piedmont, Italy

Giovanni Battista Tinetti
B: 14 Jul 1825 Torino, Italy
M: 27 May 1846 Piemonte, Italy
D: 11 Oct 1904 Italy

Luigi Bartolomeo Pastore
B: 16 Sep 1769 Piemonte, Italy
D: 7 Jul 1837 Piemonte, Italy

Maria Magdalena Pastore
B: 21 Sep 1790 Piedmont, Italy
M: 11 Feb 1805 Piemonte, Italia
D: 22 Oct 1865 Piedmont, Italy

Giovanna Motto
B: 12 May 1772 Piemonte, Italia
D: 26 Aug 1817 Piemonte, Italia

Angelina Margherita Tinetti
B: 5 Dec 1871 Piemonte, Italy
M: 02 JUN 1891 Hurley, Iron, Wisconsin, USA
D: 10 Jun 1947 Renton, King, Washington

Carlo Zanotti
B: 8 Apr 1764 Piedmont, Italy
D: Dec 1809 Piemonte, Italy

Secondo Zanotti
B: abt 1803 Piemonte, Italy
M: 9 Feb 1828 Piemonte, Italy
D: 21 Dec 1838 Piemonte, Italy

Domenica Pastore
B: 7 Aug 1753 Piedmont, Italy
D: Unknown Piedmont, Italy

Maria Catterina Zanotti-Cussio
B: 26 Jan 1830 Piemonte, Italy
M: 27 May 1846 Piemonte, Italy
D: 12 Feb 1915

Giacomo Antonio Cussio
B: 15 Feb 1778 Piemonte, Italy
D:

Maria Teresia Cussio
B: 7 May 1807 Piemonte, Italy
M: 9 Feb 1828 Piemonte, Italy
D: before 1846 Piemonte, Italy

Maria Catterina Henrico
B: 7 Mar 1779 Piemonte, Italy
D: before 1810 Piemonte, Italy

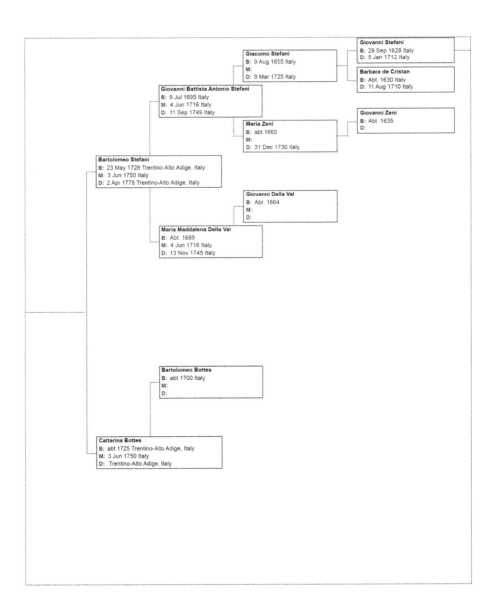

Giovanni Stefani
B: 29 Sep 1628 Italy
D: 5 Jan 1712 Italy

Giacomo Stefani
B: 9 Aug 1655 Italy
M:
D: 9 Mar 1725 Italy

Barbara de Cristan
B: Abt. 1630 Italy
D: 11 Aug 1710 Italy

Giovanni Battista Antonio Stefani
B: 9 Jul 1695 Italy
M: 4 Jun 1716 Italy
D: 11 Sep 1749 Italy

Giovanni Zeni
B: Abt. 1635
D:

Maria Zeni
B: abt 1660
M:
D: 31 Dec 1730 Italy

Bartolomeo Stefani
B: 23 May 1728 Trentino-Alto Adige, Italy
M: 3 Jun 1750 Italy
D: 2 Apr 1778 Trentino-Alto Adige, Italy

Giovanni Della Val
B: Abt. 1664
M:
D:

Maria Maddalena Della Val
B: Abt. 1689
M: 4 Jun 1716 Italy
D: 13 Nov 1745 Italy

Bartolomeo Bottes
B: abt 1700 Italy
M:
D:

Cattarina Bottes
B: abt 1725 Trentino-Alto Adige, Italy
M: 3 Jun 1750 Italy
D: Trentino-Alto Adige, Italy

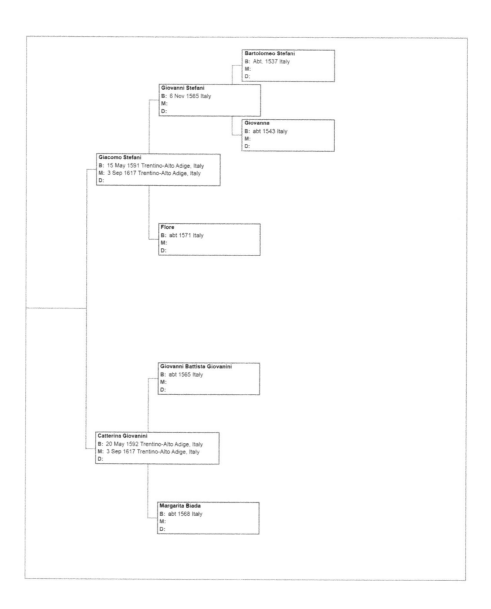

Bartolomeo Stefani
B: Abt. 1537 Italy
M:
D:

Giovanni Stefani
B: 6 Nov 1565 Italy
M:
D:

Giovanna
B: abt 1543 Italy
M:
D:

Giacomo Stefani
B: 15 May 1591 Trentino-Alto Adige, Italy
M: 3 Sep 1617 Trentino-Alto Adige, Italy
D:

Flore
B: abt 1571 Italy
M:
D:

Giovanni Battista Giovanini
B: abt 1565 Italy
M:
D:

Catterina Giovanini
B: 20 May 1592 Trentino-Alto Adige, Italy
M: 3 Sep 1617 Trentino-Alto Adige, Italy
D:

Margarita Biada
B: abt 1568 Italy
M:
D:

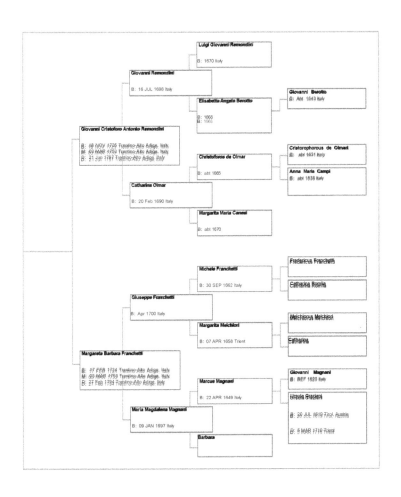

Luigi Giovanni Remondini
B: 1670 Italy

Giovanni Remondini
B: 16 JUL 1696 Italy

Giovanni Berotto
B: Abt 1643 Italy

Elisabetta Angela Berotto
B: 1668
B: 1568

Giovanni Cristoforo Antonio Remondini
B: 18 NOV 1725 Trentino-Alto Adige, Italy
M: 09 MAR 1759 Trentino-Alto Adige, Italy
B: 21 Jun 1787 Trentino-Alto Adige, Italy

Cristorophorous de Olmari
B: abt 1631 Italy

Christufsrens de Olmar
B: abt 1665

Anna Maria Campi
B: abt 1638 Italy

Catharina Olmar
B: 20 Feb 1690 Italy

Margarita Maria Caneal
B: abt 1670

Frederieva Franchetti

Michele Franchetti
B: 30 SEP 1662 Italy

Catharina Romlia

Giuseppe Franchetti
B: Apr 1700 Italy

Melchiorus Melchiori

Margarita Melchiori
B: 07 APR 1658 Trient

Catharina

Margareta Barbara Franchetti
B: 17 FEB 1734 Trentino-Alto Adige, Italy
M: 09 MAR 1759 Trentino-Alto Adige, Italy
B: 27 Feb 1794 Trentino-Alto Adige, Italy

Giovanni Magnani
B: BEF 1620 Italy

Marcus Magnani
B: 22 APR 1649 Italy

Ursula Graziani
B: 20 JUL 1619 Tirol, Austria

Maria Magdalena Magnani
B: 09 JAN 1697 Italy

B: 5 MAR 1718 Trient

Barbara

235

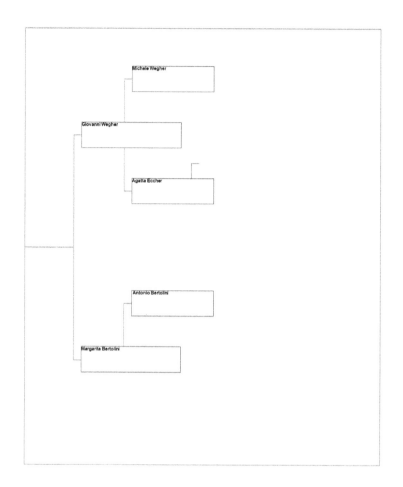

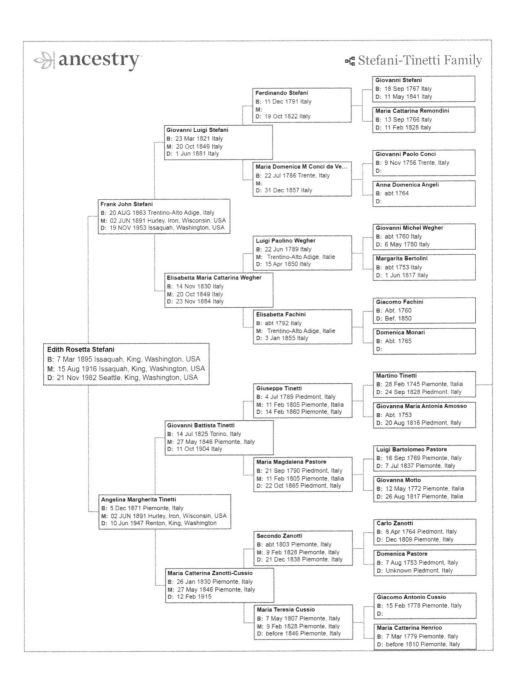

ancestry

Stefani-Tinetti Family

Giovanni Stefani
B: 18 Sep 1767 Italy
D: 11 May 1841 Italy

Ferdinando Stefani
B: 11 Dec 1791 Italy
M:
D: 19 Oct 1822 Italy

Maria Cattarina Remondini
B: 13 Sep 1766 Italy
D: 11 Feb 1828 Italy

Giovanni Luigi Stefani
B: 23 Mar 1821 Italy
M: 20 Oct 1849 Italy
D: 1 Jun 1881 Italy

Giovanni Paolo Conci
B: 9 Nov 1756 Trente, Italy
D:

Maria Domenica M Conci da Ve...
B: 22 Jul 1786 Trente, Italy
M:
D: 31 Dec 1857 Italy

Anna Domenica Angeli
B: abt 1764
D:

Frank John Stefani
B: 20 AUG 1863 Trentino-Alto Adige, Italy
M: 02 JUN 1891 Hurley, Iron, Wisconsin, USA
D: 19 NOV 1953 Issaquah, Washington, USA

Giovanni Michel Wegher
B: abt 1760 Italy
D: 6 May 1780 Italy

Luigi Paolino Wegher
B: 22 Jun 1789 Italy
M: Trentino-Alto Adige, Italie
D: 15 Apr 1850 Italy

Margarita Bertolini
B: abt 1753 Italy
D: 1 Jun 1817 Italy

Elisabetta Maria Cattarina Wegher
B: 14 Nov 1830 Italy
M: 20 Oct 1849 Italy
D: 23 Nov 1884 Italy

Giacomo Fachini
B: Abt. 1760
D: Bef. 1850

Elisabetta Fachini
B: abt 1792 Italy
M: Trentino-Alto Adige, Italie
D: 3 Jan 1855 Italy

Domenica Monari
B: Abt. 1765
D:

Edith Rosetta Stefani
B: 7 Mar 1895 Issaquah, King, Washington, USA
M: 15 Aug 1916 Issaquah, King, Washington, USA
D: 21 Nov 1982 Seattle, King, Washington, USA

Martino Tinetti
B: 28 Feb 1745 Piemonte, Italia
D: 24 Sep 1828 Piedmont, Italy

Giuseppe Tinetti
B: 4 Jul 1789 Piedmont, Italy
M: 11 Feb 1805 Piemonte, Italia
D: 14 Feb 1860 Piemonte, Italy

Giovanna Maria Antonia Amosso
B: Abt. 1753
D: 20 Aug 1816 Piedmont, Italy

Giovanni Battista Tinetti
B: 14 Jul 1825 Torino, Italy
M: 27 May 1846 Piemonte, Italy
D: 11 Oct 1904 Italy

Luigi Bartolomeo Pastore
B: 16 Sep 1769 Piemonte, Italy
D: 7 Jul 1837 Piemonte, Italy

Maria Magdalena Pastore
B: 21 Sep 1790 Piedmont, Italy
M: 11 Feb 1805 Piemonte, Italia
D: 22 Oct 1865 Piedmont, Italy

Giovanna Motto
B: 12 May 1772 Piemonte, Italia
D: 26 Aug 1817 Piemonte, Italia

Angelina Margherita Tinetti
B: 5 Dec 1871 Piemonte, Italy
M: 02 JUN 1891 Hurley, Iron, Wisconsin, USA
D: 10 Jun 1947 Renton, King, Washington

Carlo Zanotti
B: 8 Apr 1764 Piedmont, Italy
D: Dec 1809 Piemonte, Italy

Secondo Zanotti
B: abt 1803 Piemonte, Italy
M: 9 Feb 1828 Piemonte, Italy
D: 21 Dec 1838 Piemonte, Italy

Domenica Pastore
B: 7 Aug 1753 Piedmont, Italy
D: Unknown Piedmont, Italy

Maria Catterina Zanotti-Cussio
B: 26 Jan 1830 Piemonte, Italy
M: 27 May 1846 Piemonte, Italy
D: 12 Feb 1915

Giacomo Antonio Cussio
B: 15 Feb 1778 Piemonte, Italy
D:

Maria Teresia Cussio
B: 7 May 1807 Piemonte, Italy
M: 9 Feb 1828 Piemonte, Italy
D: before 1846 Piemonte, Italy

Maria Catterina Henrico
B: 7 Mar 1779 Piemonte, Italy
D: before 1810 Piemonte, Italy

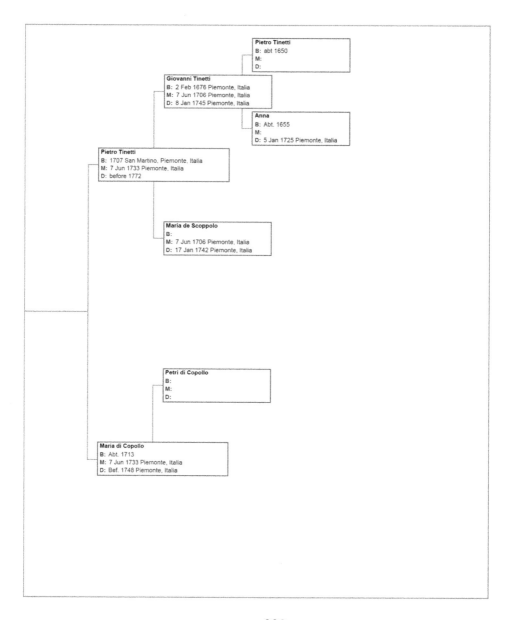

Pietro Tinetti
B: abt 1650
M:
D:

Giovanni Tinetti
B: 2 Feb 1676 Piemonte, Italia
M: 7 Jun 1706 Piemonte, Italia
D: 8 Jan 1745 Piemonte, Italia

Anna
B: Abt. 1655
M:
D: 5 Jan 1725 Piemonte, Italia

Pietro Tinetti
B: 1707 San Martino, Piemonte, Italia
M: 7 Jun 1733 Piemonte, Italia
D: before 1772

Maria de Scoppolo
B:
M: 7 Jun 1706 Piemonte, Italia
D: 17 Jan 1742 Piemonte, Italia

Petri di Copollo
B:
M:
D:

Maria di Copollo
B: Abt. 1713
M: 7 Jun 1733 Piemonte, Italia
D: Bef. 1748 Piemonte, Italia

The Stefani Family

In *Sulle Sponde Dello Sporeggio*, Pietro Micheli says that Stefani (also de Stefan and de Stefanis) is one of the oldest families in Sporminore.[1] I found them in the first parish records as noted below. The records also show a Romedio di Stefan son of Giovanni Battista marrying in 1559 and other Stefanis who I have not been able to fit in with the family. Several say "di Vigo" so it is possible the family came from Vigo Meano at that time.

1. Bartolomeo Stefani, b. abt. 1540, m. Giovanna, b. abt. 1543 probably both born in Sporminore. They baptized two children per the first parish records started after the Council of Trent decreed they should be kept.

2. i. Floriana, b. 7 Feb 1563 in Sporminore.

+3. ii. Giovanni Stefani

4. iii. Giovanni Antonio, b. abt 1567 Sporminore, m. Domenica, b. abt 1570, Children: Lucia, Bartolomeo

3. Giovanni Stefani, b. 6 Nov 1565 in Sporminore, married Flore, b. abt. 1571. N.f.r.

5. iv. Maria Stefani, b. abt 1589, m. Pero Volmar 26 Sep 1603 Sporminore (see Olmar family)

+6. v. Giacomo Stefani

7. i. Margaretta Stefani, b. 28 May 1592 in Sporminore.

6. Giacomo Stefani, b. 15 May 1591 in Sporminore, married Catterina Giovanini, b. 20 May 1592 in Sporminore, d/o Giovanni Battista Giovanini and Margarita Biada. They also had a son, Giovanni, b. 19 Nov 1590 in Sporminore.

8. vii. Maria Stefani, b. 13 Dec 1622 in Sporminore. N.f.r.

+9. viii. Giovanni Stefani

10. ix. Giovanni Battista Stefani, b. 13 Jan 1635 in Sporminore. N.f.r.

9. Giovanni Stefani, b. 29 Sep 1628 in Sporminore, married Barbara de Cristan, b. abt. 1630, d. 11 Aug 1710 in Sporminore. Giovanni d. 5 Jan 1712 in Sporminore.

+11. x. Giacomo Stefani

11. Giacomo Stefani, b. 9 Aug 1655 in Sporminore, m. abt 1681, Maria Zeni. Giacomo d. 3 Mar 1725 and Maria d. 3 Dec 1730. In some records including the marriage of his son, Giovanni Battista, the word "Magnifici" appears before Giacomo's name, this signifies that he was a master craftsman or artisan.

12. xi. Giovanni, b. abt. 1683 in Sporminore, d. 9 Sep 1733 in Sporminore. N.f.r.

13. xii. Antonia, b. 24 Aug 1684 in Sporminore. N.f.r.

14. xiii. Giacomo Antonio Guidofalco, b. 4 Aug 1685 in Sporminore, m. 10 Feb 1705, Elisabetta Zanet b. abt 1687. They had a daughter, Anna, d. 14 Mar 1734. N.f.r.

15. xiv. Catharina, b. 1 Jan 1688, m. Carlos di Villa 16 Apr 1704, n.f.r.

16. xv. Maria Magdalena, b. 19 Jun 1689 in Sporminore, m. Bartolomeo Maines, 30 Jan 1709 inn Sporminore. N.f.r.

17. xvi. Maria Margaretha, b. 15 Jan 1691 in Sporminore.

18. xvii. Anna Maria Margaretha, b. 7 Mar 1692 in Sporminore. N.f.r.

+19. xviii Giovanni Battista Antonio

20. xix Maria Domenica, b. 25 Mar 1698 in Sporminore.

19. Giovanni Battista Antonio Stefani, b. 9 Jul 1695 in Sporminore, m. Maria Maddalena Della Val b. abt 1689 in Enno, d/o Giovanni Della Val "of Enno," Maddalena died 13 Nov 1745 in Sporminore and Giovanni died 11 Sep 1749 also in Sporminore. In her death notice in the parish records they were both given the honorific "Don" and "Dona" which suggests that they held high status in the community.

21. xx. Adelaide, b. 20 Jun 1717 in Sporminore, n.f.r.

22. xxi. Daniele, b. abt 1718, d. 6 May 1719 in Sporminore.

23. xxii. Giovanni Giacomo Maximilliano, b. 18 Sep 1719 in Sporminore, d. 24 Jul 1766 in Sporminore, n.f.r.

24. xxiii. Pietro Giacomo Vigilio Domenico Antonio, b. 10 Jun 1721 in Sporminore. N.f.r.

25. xxiv. Catharina, b. 25 Mar 1724 in Sporminore,

26. xxv. Giovanni Battista Antonio, b. 14 May 1725 in Sporminore, d. 27 Oct 1754 in Sporminore. N.f.r.

27. xxvi. Francesco Antonio Vigilio, b. 22 Feb 1726 in Sporminore, n.f.r.

+28. xxvii. Bartolomeo

29. xxviii. Tomas Antonio, b. 1 Feb 1729 in Sporminore

30. xxix. Julio, b. 2 Aug 1733, d. 1 Feb 1734 in Sporminore.

31. xxx. Giuseppe, b. 2 May 1737 in Sporminore,

32. xxxi. Maria Maddalena, b. unk. d. 17 Sep 1771 in Sporminore, n.f.r.

28. Bartolomeo, b. 23 May 1728 in Sporminore, m. Catharina Bottes, b. abt. 1725 in Mezzolombardo, d/o Bartolomeo Bottes. Bartolomeo Stefani d. 2 Apr 1778 "age 50" in Sporminore

33. xxxii. Bartolomeo Antonio Valentino, b. 14 Feb 1751 in Sporminore, m. Maria Maddalena Cristan (see Cristan family). Their son, Giovanni Antonio, b. 7 Aug 1791 in Sporminore, m. Maddalena Rigotti, b. 22 Jul 1792 in Sporminore. Their children were Maddalena Catarina, b. 28 Apr 1813, m. Giovanni Antonio Cristan (see Cristan family), d. 1864 in Sporminore, Angela Carolina Cattarina b. 9 Jul 1836, Girachino Giovanni Antonio, b. 24 Apr 1840, m. Catterina Tenaglia 7 Nov 1863, Teresa Crescenza, b. 6 Jun 1844, m. Giovanni Formolo, Girachino Francesco, b. 5 May 1846, d. 29 Sep 1846, Girachino, b. 7 Sep 1851, Giovanni Fortunato, b. 3 Jan 1854, m. Guidetta Parolini.

34. xxxiii. Maria Maddalena Catharina, b. abt 1753 in Sporminore, d. 26 Oct 1761 in Sporminore.

35. xxxiv. Maria Margarita Domenica, b. abt 1756 in Sporminore, d. 23 Aug 1775 in Sporminore.

36. xxxv. Maddalena Catharina, b. unk, d. 3 Sep 1762

+37. xxxvi. Giovanni

37. Giovanni Stefani, b. 18 Sep 1767 in Sporminore, m. Maria Caterina Remondini (see Remondini family), b. 13 Sep 1766, m. 13 Jun 1788 in Sporminore, Maria d. 11 Feb 1828 in Sporminore, Giovanni d. 11 May 1841 in Sporminore.

38. xxxvii. Margarita, b. 30 Jun 1790 in Sporminore, m. in 1809, Bartolo Dallago, s/o Cristano Dallago and Barbara Zoanetti, they had a daughter, Catherine Ellena, b. 13 Aug 1822 in Sporminore, d. 4 Mar 1902.

+39. xxxviii. Ferdinando

40. xxxix. Stefano, b. 7 Aug 1794 in Sorminore, m. Maria Domenica DeCristan on 17 Feb 1813, she was b. abt. 1793, d/o Giovanni DeCristan. She died 18 May 1851 in Sporminore, he died before her. N.f.r.

41. xl. Pietro Giovanni, b. 28 Jul 1799, n.f.r.

42. xli. Catterina Barbara, b. 1 Jul 1802, m. Francesco Giovanni Nardelli, b. 10 Oct 1787 in Sporminore, m. abt. 1819. Fifteen children. N.f.r.

43. xlii. Barbara Maddalena, b. 20 Sep 1804 in Sporminore, n.f.r.

44. xliii. Domenica Clementina, b. 5 Dec 1808 in Sporminore, n.f.r.

39. Ferdinando Stefani, b. 11 Dec 1791 in Sporminore, m. Maria Domenica Maddalena Conci Da Vervo, b. 22 Jul 1786 in Torra, Taio, Trento (see Conci family), m. abt 1820 in Torra, Ferdinando d. 19 Oct 1822 of a malignant fever ("febre maligna"). Maddalena m2d. Guiseppe Weber of Mezzolombardo, 10 Feb 1824. They had four children, Guiseppe, Luigi, Elisabetta and Maria Rosa. Maddalena d. 31 Dec 1857 in Mezzolombardo.

+45. xliv. Giovanni Luigi

45. Giovanni Luigi Stefani, b. 23 Mar 1821, bp. 24 Mar 1821 in Sporminore, m. Elisabetta Maria Cattarina

Wegher, b. 14 Nov 1830 (see Wegher family), m. 20 Oct 1849 in Sporminore. Giovanni d. 1 Jun 1881, Catterina d. 23 Nov 1884 in Sporminore.

46. xlv. Giovanni Luigi Ferdinando, b. 15 Aug 1850 in Sporminore, d. 27 Jul 1861 in Sporminore.

47. xlvi. Maria Elisabetta, b. 16 May 1852 in Sporminore, d. 8 Jul 1852 in Sporminore.

48. xlvii. Adelaide Maria Anna, b. 29 Aug 1853 in Sporminore, m. Federico Friedle,s/o Pietro Friedle and Domenica, b. 25 Oct 1858 in Folgaria, Trento, m. 27 Aug 1887 in Sporminore, she died 4 Mar 1900 in Sporminore. Federico m2d, Fortunata Oscari in 1900. Children of Adelaide and Federico: Guido Luigi, b. 30 Aug 1888, m. Itala Franzoi abt 1915, d. 1921, Anonimo, b. 21 Sep 1889, d. 21 Sep 1889, Bianca Maria, b. 9 Feb 1891, d. 11 Feb 1891, Onorio Guiseppe, b. 10 Jul 1892, n.f.r., Elmo Giovanni Quino, b. 9 May 1897, d. 16 Aug 1897, Orazio Firmo Luigi, b. 24 Nov 1899, m. Guiseppina Antonia Odorizzi abt 1930, d. 9 Jul 1987.

49. xlviii. Giacomo Giovanni, b. 14 Jul 1855 in Sporminore, d. 20 Jan 1867 in Sporminore.

50. xlix. Luigia Maddalena, b. 3 Dec 1857 in Sporminore, d. 3 Jul 1859 in Sporminore.

51. l. Teresa Marianna, b. 3 Jul 1860 in Sporminore, d. 8 Feb 1863 in Sporminore.

+52. li. Francesco Giovanni (Frank John)

52. Francesco Giovanni (Frank John) Stefani, b. 20 Aug 1863 in Sporminore, m. Angelina Margarita Tinetti (see Tinetti Family), b. 5 Dec 1871, Torre Canavese, Torino, Italy, m. 2 Jun 1891, Hurley, Iron, Wisconsin, U.S.A., she d. 10 Jun 1947 Renton, King, Washington, U.S.A, Frank d. 19 Nov 1953 in Issaquah, King, Washington, U.S.A.

53. lii. Fredrick Frank Stefani (Stefan), b. 12 Apr 1892 Comox, British Columbia, Canada, m. Nellie Elisabeth Brown, b. 22 Jan 1893 Sedro-Woolley, Skagit, Washington, U.S.A., d/o Ira L. Brown and Mary Melissa Wicker, d. 20 Mar 1946, Seattle, King, Washington, U.S.A. He d. 9 Mar 1969 Seattle, King, Washington, U.S.A.

54. Arthur Frederick Stefan, b. 10 Jan 1913 Acme, Whatcom, Washington, m. Bertha Pauline Boeger, d/o William Frederick Boeger and Josephine Randina Figenschau, b. 15 Apr 1906 East Grand Forks, Polk, Minnesota, m. 8 May 1937 Seattle, King, Washington. She d. 9 Jun 2004 Snohomish, Snohomish, Washington, Arthur d. 13 Mar 1976 Cathedral City, Riverside, California

55. Elizabeth Josephine, m. Nicholas J. Collatos,

56. Dorothy Marie Stefan, b. 1 Mar 1914 Issaquah, King, Washington, m. Benson Ezra Peterson, s/o Alvin Ola Peterson and Bertha Ann Benson, b. 20 Jun 1907 St. Charles, Bear Lake, Idaho, m. 1 Mar 1935, Seattle, King, Washington, Benson d. 6 May 1982, Edmonds, Snohomish, Washington, Dorothy d. 31 Jan 2012, Edmonds, Snohomish, Washington.

57. Carol Ann Peterson

58. Maxine Elizabeth Stefan, b. 27 Apr 1915 Issaquah, King, Washington, m. Arthur Edward Ammerman, s/o Lawrence Edward Ammerman and Bertha Ellen Long, b. 10 Nov 1909 Mystic, Sullivan, Missouri, m. 22 Sep 1935 Seattle,

King, Washington, d. 25 Jan 1994 Seattle, King, Washington, Maxine d. 10 Apr 1987 Seattle, King, Washington

59. Gary A. Ammerman, m. Judith E. Pedersen, d/o Henry P. Pedersen and Pearl Hemphill, n.f.r.

60. Sandra Gay Ammerman, b. 28 May 1940 Seattle, King, Washington, m1., Le Von F. Smiley, m2., Harlan M. Snyder, m3 Roger M. De Lorm, Jr., she died 8 Nov 2006 Gig Harbor, Pierce, Washington

61. Virginia Mae Stefan, b. 10 May 1916 Seattle, King, Washington, m1., Myron Charles Miller, s/o Charles Fremont Miller and Caroline Coss, b. 2 Feb 1899 Brinnon, Jefferson, Washington, m. 12 Oct 1936 Seattle, King, Washington, d. 15 may 1968 Seattle, king, Washington, m2., H. Lester Gould, s/o Harry Sesler Morehead Gould and Susan Ellen Bradbury, b. 28 Jan 1895 Patterson, Passaic, New Jersey, m. 28 Apr 1973 Seattle, King, Washington, d. 20 Jun 1984, Virginia d. 26 May 2008 Gig Harbor, Pierce, Washington no issue

62. Jack Cushman Stefan, b. 17 Jun 1922 Seattle, King, Washington, d. 12 Oct 1936 Seattle, King, Washington

63. Bernice Jean "Babe" Stefan, b. 21 Aug 1924 Seattle, King, Washington, m. Cecil LeRoy Lemen, s/o James Gibson Lemen and Ethel Maude Brownlee, b. 11 Jun 1921 Topeka, Shawnee, Kansas, m. 20 May 1942 Yuma, Yuma. Arizona, d. 3 Aug 1955 Myrtle Creek, Douglas, Oregon. She died 3 Aug 1955 Myrtle Creek, Douglas, Oregon

64. Peggy Jean Lemen, m. Philip Samuel Goldenman, div.

65. Marissa N. Goldenman, m. Douglas A. Fleckenstein.

66. liii. John Frank, b. 27 Aug 1893 Issaquah, King, Washington, U.S.A., d. Feb 1898, Issaquah, King, Washington, U.S.A.

+67. liv. Edith Rosetta

68. lv. Adelina Justina, b. 29 Nov 1896 Issaquah, King, Washington, U.S.A.m1st, John Burr Adams b. 17 Jul 1894 Rockville, Park, Indianna, U.S.A., m. 22 Mar 1916

Seattle, King, Washington, U.S.A., div. 1927 Seattle, King, Washington, U.S.A., d. 16 Apr 1950 Seattle, King, Washington, U.S.A., m2d Frank Carl Dorner, b. 10 Mar 1901Kansan City, Jackson, Missouri, U.S.A. s/o Andrew Dorner and Bertha Radtke, m. 2 Jun 1934 Seattle, King, Washington, U.S.A., d. 29 Nov 1985 Seattle, King, Washington, U.S.A. Adelina d. 18 Jul 1995 Bremerton, Kitsap, Washington

Children by John Burr Adams:

69. Harold Lewis, b. 9 Feb 1917 Seattle, King, Washington, U.S.A. m. Dawn Satterlee, b. 18 Sep 1917 Marshfield, Wisconsin, U.S.A., d/o Clarence M. Satterlee and Beulah Mason, m. 3 Jun 1939 Tacoma, Pierce, Washington, U.S.A., div. 1958 Seattle, King, Washington, U.S.A., m2d David Giles Crosby b. 23 Oct 1924 Franklin Co., Ohio, d. 9 Apr 2005 Centralia, Lewis, Washngton, U.S.A.

70. Patricia, n.f.r.

71. Paul Lewis, m. Jacqueline Marie Stuve, n.f.r.

72. Judy, n.f.r.

Harold m2d Frances Ellen Sallee and m3d Nevalyn M. Schubert. Dawn d.22 Nov 2003 Centralia, Lewis, Washington, U.S.A. Harold d. 15 May 2004 Grant's Pass, Josephine, Oregon, U.S.A.

73. Samuel John, b. 3 Nov 1918, Seattle, King, Washington, U.S.A., m. Harmony M. Durkee, b. 4 Oct 1919, Wausau, Marathon, Wisconsin, U.S.A. d/o Floyd Allen Durkee and Stella Peck, m. 2 Apr 1939, Seattle, King, Washington, U.S.A. She d. 15 Sep 2005 I Seattle, King, Washington, U.S.A. and he d. 23 Aug 2006 in Lynnwood, Snohomish, Washington, U.S.A. Their children were:

74. Donald Leroy, m. Karen Sue Johnston, d/o C. Edward and Evangeline Johnston, div, m2 Andrea

75. Stephen Todd

76. Julie K. m. Jason B. Alphounson.

77. Richard Todd, b. 7 Jun 1944, Seattle, King, Washington, d. 15 Mar 1964 Seattle, King, Washington

78. David Alan, m1., Edwina Joy Johnston, d/o C. Edward and Evangeline Johnston, div, m2. Rebecca Lynn Nichols, div, m3 Kristi

79. Michael L

80. lvi. Mary Victoria, b. 14 Mar 1900 Issaquah, King, Washington, U.S.A., m. Eric Emanuel (Andersson) b. 12 Nov 1884 Medaker, Vastmanland, Sweden s/o Karl Olaf Andersson and Anna Lovisa Ersdotter, m. 30 Mar 1918 Issaquah, King, Washington, U.S.A., d. 29 Mar 1975 Bellevue, King, Washington, U.S.A. Mary d. 5 Feb 1994 Bremerton, Kitsap, Washington, U.S.A. Children:

81. Anita Mae Emanuel, b. 28 Sep 1918 Issaquah, King, Washington, U.S.A. m. Charles Edwin Holt b. 18 Jul 1917, Caruthers, Fresno, California, U.S.A., s/o Charles Edwin Holt and Jenny Victoria Latt, m. 18 Feb 1940 Seattle, King, Washington, U.S.A., d. 9 Aug 1995 Seabeck, Kitsap, Washington, U.S.A. Anita d. 31 Aug 2003 Belfair, Mason, Washington, U.S.A. Children:

82.Merna Mae Holt, m. Russel Peter "Pete" Endsley, s/o George Russel Endsley and Helen Lousie Rassmussen.

83. Mark Fleming Endsley, m. Patricia A. Thompson.

84. Ryan Michael Endsley

85. Eric James Endsley

86. Victoria Ann "Vicki" Holt, m1., Edward Gomez, m2., Geoffrey D. Hiatt, div.

87. Merry Lee Holt, m. Richard Quy, s/o Harvey F. Quy and Delores Johnson.

88. Cheryl Lynn Quy, m. Henry Fred Sucharski.

89. Kyle Sucharski

90. Scott Eric Quy, b. 13 Aug 196, m. Lori Ann Hunsaker.

91. William Charles Holt m1., Virginia Mae Davis, d/o James Albert Davis, Jr. and Marian Francis Dever, div. m2., Linda J. Maguire, div. m3. Sharon Johnson.

92. Anthony J. Holt

93. Andrew C. Holt

94. Carl Frank, b. 25 Jul 1921 Issaquah, King, Washington, U.S.A., d. 3 Oct 1972 Seattle, King, Washington, U.S.A.

95. lvii. Francis Eugene George, b. 29 Apr 1904 in Issaquah, King, Washington, U.S.A. d. 24 Jan 1908 in Issaquah, King, Washington.

96. lviii. Clement Eugene, b. 1 Mar 1908, Issaquah, King, Washington, U.S.A. m. Pietje (Peechie) Bergsma, b. 13 Feb 1908, Akkrum, Friesland, Netherlands, d/o Henry Tjeerd Bergsma and Harmke Venema. He died 7 Jul 1977 Issaquah, King, Washington, U.S.A. and she died. 20 Dec 2003 Issaquah, King, Washington, U.S.A. Children:

97. Marian Mae Stefani, b. 29 May 1931 Issaquah, King, Washington, m. Kenneth Lee Hampton, s/o Lawrence Syvester Hampton and Lydia Wolff, b. 12 Nov 1931 Emerson, Faulk, South Dakota, m. 22 Dec 1956 Issaquah, King, Washington, d. 31 Oct 2020

98. Gregory Charles Hampton, b. 19 Mar 1958 Issaquah, King, Washington, m. Barbara Ellen Risdon, d/o Lester Edmond Dale and Helen J. Hammond, Gregory d. 6 Jul 2003 Issaquah, King, Washington

99. Lisa M. Hampton, m. Daniel T. Studley, div.

100. Daniel Kenneth Hampton

101. Gary Lee Hampton

102. Gordon Kenneth Hampton

103. John Frank Stefani, m1 Margaret J. Clark, d/o Maurice Paul Clark and Ann Florine O'Neil, b. 16 May 1941 Havre, Hill, Montana, div. She died12 Sep 1998 New Castle, King, Washington, m2., Gail J. Van Demoere.

104. Edith Rosetta Stefani, b. 7 Mar 1895 Issaquah, King, Washington, U.S.A., m. Lucas Carlisle Kells, b. 17 Jun 1882 Melrose, Stearns, Minnesota, U.S.A., s/o Stephen Avery Kells and Isabella Duncan, m. 15 Aug 1916 Issaquah, King, Washington, U.S.A., d. 6 Oct 1946 Fort Steilacoom, Pierce, Washington, U.S.A. Edith d. 21 Nov 1982, Seattle, King, Washington, U.S.A.

105. lix. Lyman Francis, b. 19 May 1917 Seattle, King, Washington, U.S.A. m. Barbara Scovil Wright, b. 14 May 1923 Sacramento, Sacramento, California, U.S.A. d/o Mark Hatfield Wright and Leila Scovil, m. 31 Aug 1946 New York, New York, New York, U.S.A., div. about 1955, m2d Alan Starke, m3d Valiante, d. 9 Oct 2010 Sarasota, Sarasota, Florida, U.S.A. He died 4 Nov 2004, Seattle, King, Washington, U.S.A. Children:

106. Leila Stefani Kells, m. Charles M "Carlos" Newcomb, div.

107. Jason Newcomb, m. Jennifer B

108. Aurora Newcomb

109. Elena Anastasia Newcomb

110. Apollo Newcomb

111. Christina Valerie Kells, m. Ronald Cohen, div.

112. Sean M. Cohen

+113. Lx. Margaret Edith (twin)

114. lxi. Milton Carlisle, (twin) m. Kathleen Mary Sheehan, d/o Raymond Edward Sheehan and Lydia E. Fuerst, div, m2d Donald Davenport Children:

115. Lawrence Carlisle Kells

116. Kathleen E Kells, m. Pavel Curtis

Milton m2d JoAnne Dexter b. 26 Jun 1928 Los Angeles, Los Angeles, California, U.S.A. d/o Nelson James E Dexter and Charline Pearl Brizzolari, m. 7 Dec 1962 Palo Alto. San Mateo, California, U.S.A. d. 9 Jun 2013 Cincinnati, Hamilton, Ohio, U.S.A. Milton. d. 16 Dec 1996 Seattle, King, Washington, U.S.A.

117. Beth Aileen Kells, m. Mark William DuBois, s/o William H. and Mary Ellen DuBois

118. Steven DuBois

119. David DuBois

120. lxii. Doris Muriel, b. 27 Sep 1923 Seattle, King, Washington, U.S.A. m. Alfred Hornung b. 18 Feb 1904 Switzerland s/o Samuel Hornung and Anna Hoeuing, m. 29

Sep 1973 New York, New York, New York, U.S.A. d. 21 Mar 1992 Brooklyn, Kings, New York U.S.A. Doris d. 24 Feb 2000 Seattle, King, Washington, U.S.A. d.s.p.

113. Margaret Edith Kells (twin) b. 7 May 1920 Seattle, King, Washington, U.S.A. m. John Marshall Peterson b. 6 Jan 1922 Ft. Worth, Tarrant, Texas, U.S.A. s/o Walter Leonard Peterson and Elizabeth Hudson m. 30 Jan 1943 Seattle, King, Washington, div.22 Sep 1959 Little Rock, Pulaski, Arkansas, U.S.A. m2d Betty LaVerne Gutteridge 1 Feb 1960 Little Rock, Pulaski, Arkansas, U.S.A., John d. 14 Apr 1985 Athens,, Athens, Ohio, U.S.A., LaVerne d. 13 Nov 1995 Athens, Athens, Ohio, U.S.A. Margaret m2d Arthur Leon "Mac" McDonald b. 29 Aug 1919 Oroville, Okanogan, Washington, U.S.A. s/o Leon Francis McDonald and Isabelle Maude Weir, m. 20 Sep 1969 Tukwila, King, Washington, U.S.A., d. 8 May 2012 Des Moines, King, Washington, U.S.A. Margaret d. 5 Dec 1999 Tukwila, King, Washington, U.S.A.

+121. lxiii. Wendy Leigh Peterson,

122. lxiv. Rhonda Gay, b. 12 Nov 1951 East Riverdale, Prince George's, Maryland, U.S.A. unm. d. 7 Mar 2018 Hillsboro, Washington. Oregon, U.S.A. d.s.p.

125. Wendy Leigh Peterson m. Dennis Michael Negley, s/o James Casper Negley and Eloise Margaret Knock,

,+126. Lxv. Devin Margaret Negley

127. lxvi. Sean Marshall Negley

126. Devin Margaret Negley, m, John Richard Weber, s/o Richard Lee Weber and Angela Marie Criscione,

127. lxvii.Crispin Lee

128. lxviii. Elinor Catherine

The Wegher Family

Also spelled Beger, Begher, Weger. Weger is a German surname meaning "weigher." The Wegher family came to Sporminore from Lauregno, the farthest south village in the Alta Val di Non, northwest of Sporminore.

They were blacksmith's and took over the blacksmith position at Maso Milano. The family still lives and owns restaurants in Maso Milano. This is a small clearing below Sporminore, on the banks of the Sporeggio. It was named for a man from Milan who founded the blacksmith business there. Eccher is noted by Micheli to also be spelled Hecher and pronounced "Egger." It is a German name deriving from the word "ecke" meaning corner or area or edge.

1. Michele Wegher, b. abt, 1710 Lauregno, Bolzano, m. Agatta Eccher, she d. 23 Apr 1780 Sporminore, Michele d. 11 Aug 1780 Sporminore.

+ii. Giovanni

iii. Giovanni Antonio, b. 21 Oct 1751 Sporminore, n.f.r.

2. Giovanni Wegher, b. abt 1738 Lauregno, m. Margareta b. abt.1740, d.24 Jun 1817 Sporminore, Giovanni d. 2 Mar 1823 Sporminore.

+iv. Giovanni Michele

v. Michele, b. 1768 Sporminore, n.f.r.

vi. Maria, b. unk Sporminore, d. 19 Oct 1752 Sporminore, n.f.r.

3.   Giovanni Michele Wegher, b. abt, 1760 Sporminore,
     m. Margareta Bertolini d/o Antonio Bertolini b. abt.
     1753 Vega, Margareta d. 1 Jun 1817 Sporminore.

vii. Cecilia, b. 1773 Sporminore, d. 13 Sep 1787
Sporminore

viii. Maria, b. 1773(twin?) Sporminore, d. 19 Oct 1781
Sporminore.

x.Maria Teresa, b. 24 Jul 1785 Sporminore, n.f.r.

+xi. Luigi Paolino

xii. Monica, b. 1790 Sporminore, d. 4 Jun 1792
Sporminore n.f.r.

xiii. Agostino, b. 25 Aug 1792 Sporminore n.f.r.

xiv. Giovanni, b. unk. d. 6 May 1780 Sporminore n.f.r.

4.   Luigi Paolino Wegher, b. 22 Jun 1789
     Sporminore, m. Elisabetta Fachini, b. abt. 1792 Vigo
     Meano, d/o Giacomo Facchini (see Facchini Family)
     and Domenica Monari, d.3 Jan 1855 Sporminore,
     Luigi d. 15 Apr 1850 Sporminore.

xv. Giovanni Vincenzo, b. 20 May 1812 Sporminore,

xvi. Giovanni Luigi, b. 15 May 1816, m. Anna Franzoi,
b. abt. 1826, d/o Lorenzo Franzoi and Liliargareta Paizzardi,

xvii. Giacomo Giovanni, b. 10 Jan 1819 Sporminore, m. Teresa Zanon, he d. 17 Aug 1868, they had fourteen children.

xviii. Giovanni Francesco, b. 18 Jul 1820, d. abt. 1821

xix. Giovanni Francesco, b. 20 Dec 1821 Sporminore, m. Teresa Moresco, d/o Giovanni Moresco and Cattarina Kollama, b. 26 Feb 1825 Spormaggiore, m. 11 Feb 1826 Spormaggiore, d. 29 Feb 1880 Sporminore. Giovanni d. 24 Dec 1884 Sporminore, they had nine children. He also had a daughter, Anna, b. 1864, d. 25 Jan 1863, by Catterina Zancanella.

xx. Teresa Maria Luigia, b. 1 Nov 1823 Sporminore,

xxi. Giuglio Fortunato, b. 22 Oct 1825 Sporminore, m. Margareta Franzoi, he d. 10 Jun 1905 Sporminore. Child: Guilio, b. 1860 Sporminore, m. Monica Remondini (see Monica Remondini line) 14 Apr 1888 Sporminore, b. 2 Feb 1869, d. 1931 Sporminore, they had eight children.

xxii. Celeste Nicolo, b. 15 Nov 1827 Sporminore, m. Orsola Carli b. abt. 1830, Celeste d. 23 Jun 1898 Sporminore, child: Luigi Celeste b. 18 Jan 1862 Spormaggiore, m. Gioseffa Francesca Maria Betta, b. 27 Nov 1866 Mezzocorona

Children Joseph J., Virginia, Josephine who all died in Michigan, U.S.A.

+xxiii. Elisabetta Maria Cattarina, b. 14 Nov 1830, m. Giovanni Luigi Stefani (see Stefani Family)

The Remondini Family

In *Sulle Sponde dello Sporeggio*, Pietro Micheli says that the Remondini family at the end of 1500 from Ampez de Carnia which is Ampezza in Carnia in the Friuli-Venetia region of Italy. The Remondinis immigrated to Sporminore as weavers. The name may be German, Rein=pure, Mond=moon.

1. Luigi Giovanni Remondini, b. 1670 Sporminore, m. Elisabetta Angela Berotto b. 1668 d/o Giovanni Berotto m. 20 Jan 1693 Sporminore d. 12 Dec 1738 Sporminore Luigi d. 2 Jan 1756 Sporminore.

+2. i. Giovanni

3. ii. Anna Maria, b. 23 Sep 1701 Sporminore n.f.r.

2. Giovanni Remondini, b. 16 Jul 1698 Sporminore, m. Cattarina Olmar (see Olmar family) b. 20 Feb 1690 Sporminore, m. 19 Apr 1723 Sporminore, d. 13 Oct 1774 Sporminore. Giovanni d. 15 Aug 1757 Sporminore.

4. iii. Anna Maria, b. 5 Sep 1724 Sporminore n.f.r.

5. iv. Giacomo Cristoforo Antonio, b. 18 Sep 1725 Sporminore, n.f.r.

+6. v. Giovanni Cristoforo Antonio

7. vi. Domenica Cattarina, b. 20 Sep 1728 Sporminore, n.f.r.

8. vii. Giovanni Battista, b. 20 Oct 1731, Sporminore,

9. viii. Juliano Giovanni Battista, b. 20 Sep 1732, Sporminore, n.f.r.

10. ix. Maria Elisabetta, b. 1735 Sporminore, d. 19 Aug 1742, Sporminore

6. Giovanni Cristoforo Antonio Remondini, b. 18 Nov 1725 Sporminore, m. Margreta Barbara Franchetti, (see Franchetti Family) b. 17 Sep 1724 Torra, Taio, Trento, m. 3

Mar 1753 Torbole, Taio, Trento, d. 27 Feb 1794 Sporminore, Giovanni d. 21 Jun 1797 Sporminore

11. x. Giuseppe Germalius, b. 29 Jan 1754 Sporminore, n.f.r.

12. xi. Giovanni Antonio, b. 1 Nov 1755, Sporminore, n.f.r.

13. xii. Giovanni Cristoforo Antonio, b. 1 Sep 1757, Sporminore, m. Pasqua Endrizzi abt 1764 Cavedago, Trento, d. 12 Feb 1825 Sprominore, he d. 10 Mar 1809 Sporminore, Children: Giovanni, Sebastiano

14. xiii. Maria Cattarina, b. 1 Nov 1759 Sporminore

15. xiv. Maria Cattarina, b. 24 Sep 1761 Sporminore

16. xv. Giovanna Pietro, b. 4 Jun 1763 Sporminore, d. 6 Jan 1776 Sporminore

17. xvi. Maria Cristina, b. 13 Sep 1766 Sporminore,

+18. xvii Maria Cattarina

19. xviii. Maria Cristina, b.24 Jun 1768 Sporminore

18.Maria Cattarina Remondini, b. 13 Sep 1766 Sporminore, m. Giovanni Stefani (see Stefani family)

Remondini ancestors of Monica Remondini

13. Giovanni Cristoforo Antonio Remondini (see 13 in Remondini Family above) m. Pasqua Endrizzi

13-1 Giovanni Remondini, b. 25 Oct 1784 Sporminore, Austria, m. Claudia Teresa Franzoi, b. 16 Sep 1792, Sporminore

13-2 Giovanni Battista, b. 9 Apr 1820 Sporminore, m. Teresa Gabrielli, d/o Giacomo Gabrielli and Lucia Maria Formolo, b. 15 Jan 1826 Sporminore

13-3 Cunegonda Monica, b. 2 Feb 1869 Sporminore, m. Giulio Wegher, s/o Giulio Fortunato Wegher and Margarita Franzoi, b. 1860 Sporminore, m. 14 Apr 1888 Sporminore, Monica d. 1931 Sporminore.

Families Allied with the Remondini Family

The Olmar Family

This family is not listed in Micheli which suggests that there were none of that name still living in Sporminore in 1977. The name was originally spelled Volmar in the records. That name is of German origin meaning renowned ruler, a house of Volmar or Vollman was well known in Bavaria in the Middle Ages. In the Sporminore records it is spelled Olmar, Volmar, Olmari, de Olmaris and others.

1. Pietro de Olmari, b. abt.1550 Sporminore, m. Francesca, b. abt. 1558, n.f.r.

ii. Antonio, b. abt. 1574 Sporminore n.f.r.

+iii. Pietro, b. abt. 1576 Sporminore,

iv. Innocente Giacomo, b. 28 Dec 1578 Sporminore,

3.Pietro de Olmari, b. abt. 1576 Sporminore, m. Maria Stefani d/o Giovanni and Flore Stefani (see Stefani Family) 26 Sep 1603 Sporminore

+v. Giovanni Battista

vi. Christophel de Olmari, b. 20 Oct 1607 Sporminore, m. Maria   n.f.r., Children: Antonio b. 19 Jan 1633 Sporminore, n.f.r.

4.Giovanni Battista de Olmari, b. 15 Sep 1603, m. Barbara de Cristan, b. 7 Dec 1607 Sporminore d/o Andrea de Cristan and Maria, m. 2 Sep 1631 Sporminore, d. 11 Aug 1710 Sporminore, his d. unk.

+vii. Christophorous

viii. Pietro, b. 23 Sep 1632 Sporminore, m. Maria, b. abt. 1645, d. 14 Mar 1707 Sporminore, Pietro d. 9 Jan 1709 Sporminore Child: Barbara,, b. abt. 1670 Sporminore, m. Stefano Franzoi s/o Stefano Franzoi, 26 Jun 1690 Sporminore, son: Giovanni Battista Franzoi, b. 1 Mar 1706 Sporminore n.f.r.

ix. Anna, b. 1 Dec 1634 Sporminore n.f.r.

7. Christopherous de Olmari, b. abt. 1631 Sporminore, m. Anna Maria Campi, b. abt. 1638 Sporminore d/o Giovanni Battista Campi m. Jan 1656 Sporminore, n.f.r.

+x. Christoforos

10. Christoforos de Olmar, b. abt. 1665 Sporminore, m. Margarita Maria Canesi, b. 1670 n.f.r.

+xi. Cattarina

xii. Barbara Magdalena, b. 2 Jan 1692 Sporminore

xiii. Margarita Domenica, b. 30 Mar 1693 Sporminore, m. Tomas Pietro de Melchiori,

1Feb 1714 Sporminore, n.f.r.

11. Cattarina Olmar b. 20 Feb 1690 Sporminore, m. Giovanni Remondini (see Remondini Family)

The Franchetti Family

The name Franchetti is another that derives from a pet name for Francesco, -etti means little. They were from Torbole, located about 19 miles southwest of Trento on the shores of Lake Garda.

1. Frederico Franchetti, b. abt. 1637, m. Cattarina Romlia, b. before 1640, n.f.r.

+ii. Michele

iii. Maria Catterina, b. 11 Dec 1665, Torbole, n.f.r.

iv. Giovanni Domenico, b. 10 Jan 1672, Torbole, Michele Franchetti, b. 30 Sep 1662, Torbole or Torra m. Margarita Melchiori d/o Melchiorius Melchiori and Cattarina, b. 7 Apr 1658 Segno,Torra, m. 26 Apr 1684 Torrra, n.f.r.

v. Giovanni Frederico, b. 1685 Torra n.f.r.

vi. Anna Catterina, b. 1689 Torra, n.f.r.

vii. Giovanni Frederico, b. 1693, Torra n.f.r.

+viii. Giuseppe

ix. Giovanni Michele, b. 12 Sep 1703 Torra, m. Clara Chini, b. 9 Aug 1709 Segno, Torra, Child: Giacomo Giuseppe, b. 27 May 1745, Torra, n.f.r.

> a. Giuseppe Franchetti, b. Apr 1700, Torra, m. Maria Magdalena Magnani b. 9 Jan 1697 Torbole d/o Marco Magnani and Barbara (se Magnani Family) m. 1723 Torbole, n.f.r.

+x. Margareta Barbara

xi. Barbara Catterina Margareta, b. 20 Dec 1725, Torra, Taio n.f.r.

xii. Giacomo Michele, b. 16 Sep 1727, Torra, Taio

xiii. Giuseppe Antonio, b. 30 May 1733, Torra, Taio

2. Margreta Barbara Franchetti, b. 17 Feb 1724 Torra, Taio, m. Giovanni Cristoforo Antonio Remondini (see Remondini Family)3 Mar 1753 Torra, d. 27 Feb 1794 Sporminore.

The Melchiori Family

Micheli says that the name comes from the name of the Wise Man in the Bible. This name is found in Sporminore.

1.Giacomo Melchiori, b. abt. 1596, m. Margarita, b. abt. 1601.

+i. Melchiorus

2.Melchiorus Melchiori, b. 27 Nov 1621, Torbole, m. Cattarina, b. abt. 1626, m. 21 Feb 1647 Trento n.f.r.

ii. Daniele, b. 6 Jan 1646 Torbole, n.f.r.

iii. Antonio, b. 1647, Torbole, n.f.r.

+iv. Margareta

v. Cattarina, b. 2 Dec 1662 Torbole, n.f.r.

vi. Melchior, b. 2 May 1665 Torbole, n.f.r.

vii. Bartolomeo, b. 3 Mar 1667, Torbole, n.f.r.

3.Margareta Melchiori, b. 7 Apr 1658 Torbole, m. Michele Franchetti (see Franchetti Family) 26 Apr 1684 Torra

The Magnani Family

In *Our Italian Surnames*, Joseph G. Fucilla says that Magnani means blacksmith or locksmith.

1. Giovanni Magnani, b. before 1620 Torbole, m. Ursula Graziani d/o Giovanni Graziani, b. abt 1593 in Torra, and Anna, b. abt 1598 Torra, d. 27 Feb 1649 Segno Torra, they also had a son, Giovanni b. before 1610 Segna, Torra, d. 9 Jan 1691 Torra. Giovanni and Ursula m. 14 Feb 1638 Torbole, she died 5 Mar 1710 Torra.

ii. Valentino, b. 12 Dec 1637 Torbole, n.f.r.

iii. Maria, b. Mar 1643 Torbole, n.f.r.

iv. Giovanni Michele, b. 29 Sep 1645 Torbole

v. Giovanni Michele, b. 1648 Torbole, n.f.r.

+vi. Marco

vii. Francesco, b. 1662 Torbole, n.f.r.

  2.Marco Magnani, b. 22 Apr 1649 Torra, m.

Barbara, b. abt. 1659, n.f.r.

viii. Ursula, b. 4 Sep 1679, Torbole, n.f.r.

ix. Anna, b. 12 Jun 1683 Torbole, n.f.r.

x. Barbara, b. 1681 Torbole, n.f.r.

xi. Pietro, b. 1687 Torbole, n.f.r.

xii. Giacoma, b. May 1690 Torbole, n.f.r.

xiii. Barbara, b. 1693 Torbole, n.f.r.

+xiv. Maria Magdalena

3. Maria Magdalena Magnani, b. 9 Jan 1697

   Torbole, m. Giuseppe Franchetti (see Franchetti

   Family) 1723 Torbole

Conci Family

The Conci Family was from Torra, Taio in *Val di Non*. The name of the family is Conci, in Giovanni Luigi Stefani"s birth certificate his mother's name is given as "Conci da Vervo" indicating that she came from Vervo. The "da Vervo" designation does not appear in any other records found so far. The name Conci comes from a pet name for Francesco. "Francesconi" or "Franconi." The name is found throughout Italy.

Domenico Paolo Conci, b. abt 1730, m. Anna Maria Domenica Del Piaz, b. ab. 1732, n.f.r.

Francesco Antonio Paoli, b. 17 Feb 1752 in Torra, Taio, n.f.r.

+Giovanni Paolo

Giovanni Paolo Conci, b. 9 Nov 1756, Torra, Taio, m. Anna Domenica Angeli, b. abt. 1764 n.f.r.

Giovanni Paoli, b. 12 May 1784, Torra, Taio n.f.r.

+Maria Domenica Maddalena

Pietro Antonio Carlo, b. 26 Feb 1788, Torra, Taio n.f.r.

Nicola Ignazio, b. 1 Feb 1790, Torra, Taio, n.f.r.

    i.   Giuseppe Luigi Feliciano, b. 9 Jul 1792, Torra, Taio, n.f.r.

    ii.   Maria Catterina Modesta, b. 12 Feb 1795, Torra, Taio, n.f.r.

    iii.   Alessandro Angelo Fortunato, b. 14 Dec 1796, Torra, Taio, n.f.r.

1. Maria Domenica Maddalena Conci da Vervo (see Stefani Family)

The Facchini Family

The surname Facchini comes from the word "facia" meaning face. It is thought to have been given to someone with a striking face.

1. Giacomo Facchini, b. abt.1735, n.f.r.

+ii. Giacomo

2. Giacomo Facchini, b. abt. 1760, m. Domenica Monari, d/o Giacomo Monari, b. abt. 1765, n.f.r.

iii. Giovanni Battista, b. 6 Feb 1785, Vigo Meano,

+iv. Elisabetta

3. Elisabetta Facchini, b. abt. 1792, Vigo Meano,

m. Luigi Paolino Wegher (see Wegher Family)

Descendants of Adelaide Maria Anna Stefani and Federico Friedl

1. Guido Luigi Friedl/Fridle, b. 30 Aug 1888 Sporminore, Trentino, Italy, m. Itala Franzoi, b. 1893 Sporminore, Trentino, Italy, d. 1958 Sporminore, Trentino, Italy, Guido d. 1921.

2. Carmello Fridle, b. 1916, m. Irma Cristan, b. 1923, d. 2007, Carmello d. 1986

3. Vittorio Fridle, b. 1946, m. Daniela Bonato, b. 1950

4. Ariana Fridle, b. 1974, m. Luca Carli, b. 1969

5. Francesco Carli, b. 1999

6. Gemma Fridle, b. 1949, m. Mario Franchi

7. Martina Franchi

8. Matteo Franchi, m. Simone

9. Violante Franchi

10. Alice Franchi

11. Tiziana Fridle, b. 1953, m. Doriano Finotti

12. Sara Finotti, m.Stefano

13. Alessandra Finotti, m. Fabrizio Mantovan

14. Giulia Mantovan

15. Giacomo Mantovan

16. Vittorio Fridle, b. 1918 d. 1943

17. Daria Fridle, b. 12 Apr 1921, m. Angelo Rigotti,

b. 1910 d. 1955 Daria d. 28 Mar 2016

18. Valerio Rigotti, m. Fulvia Loner

19. Valentina Rigotti

20. Gabriella Rigotti, m. Disma Divigili

21. Ivan Divigili, m. Elena Marcolla

22. Alessia Devigili

23. Cristian Devigili

24. Giuseppina Fridle, b. 1928 m. Silvio Mattevi, b.

1921, d. 2013 Giuseppina d. 1995

25. Ugo Mattevi, b. 1955 d. 1966

26. Walter Mattevi, b. 1967 d. 1991

27. Ivo Mattevi, n.f.r.

28. Luca Mattevi

29. Silvia Mattevi

30. Anomino Friedl ,b. 21 Sep 1889, d. 21 Sep 1889 Sporminore, Trentino, Italy

31. Bianca Maria Friedl, b. 9 Feb 1891, d. 11 Feb 1891 Sporminore, Trentino, Italy

32. Onorio Giuseppe Friedl, b. 10 Jul 1892 n.f.r.

33. Elmo Giovanni Quinto Friedl, b. 9 May 1897, d. 16 Aug 1897 Sporminore, Trention, Italy

34. Orazio Firmo Luigi Friedl, b. 24 Nov 1899 Sporminore, Trentino, Italy, m. Giuseppina Antonia Odorizzi, d/o Enrico Odorizzi and Maddalena Valentini, b. 14 Mar 1904 Sporminore, Trentino, Italy, m. abt 1930, d. 11 Apr 1979 Sporminore, Trentino, Italy, Orazio Luigi d. 9 Jul 1987 Sporminore, Trention, Italy

35. Augostino Fridle. B 12 Oct 1931 Sporminore, Trentino, Italy, m. Stephany d. 31 Dec 1986 Dietikon, Zurick, Switzerland

36. Peter Fridle

37. Suzy Fridle

38. Martin

39. Enrico

40. Mchelle

41. Nicole

42. Guido Fridle, b. 27 Oct 1937 Sporminore, Trentino, Italy, d. 15 Jun 1996 Sporminore, Trentino, Italy

43. Dolores Fridle, m. Sgarbossa

44. Mauro Sgarbossa

45. Mattia Sgarbossa

46. Anna Fridle, m. Albert Kluiber

47. Patrizia Kluiber

48. Doris Kluiber

The Tinetti Family

The Tinetti name is a rare one, found mostly in the Piemonte region of Italy. It comes from the name Tino (a common pet name for men with names like Albertino, Martino, etc.) and adding "-etti" or "little."

1. Pietro Tinetti, b. abt 1650, m. Anna, b. abt 1655, d. 5 Jan 1725, San Martino, Torino n.f.r.
   +ii. Giovanni Tinetti.

2. Giovanni Tinetti, b. 2 Feb 1676 San Martino, m. Maria de Scoppolla, b. abt 1687, d. 17 Jn 1742 San Martino, n.f.r.
   iii. Pietro Tinetti

3. Pietro Tinetti, b. 1707 San Martino, m. Maria de Coppolla, b. abt 1713, d/o Pietro,d. 7 Jun 1733 San Martino, m2d. Domenica Felia Trosella, 9 Jan 1748 San Martino, d. before 1772.
   +iv.Martin Tinetti

   v. Pietro Tinetti, b, unk., his son Giovanni, d. 7 Aug 1801 Torre Canavese, n.f.r.

   vi. Giovanni Tinetti, b. unk, m. Domenica Maria, Children: Stefano, b. 9 Oct 1774 Torre Canavese, Domenica

Maria, b. 10 Jan 1780, d. 10 Jan 1782 Torre Canavese,

Martino, b. 4 Apr 1784 Torre Canavese, daughter

Giovanna, b. 10 Aug 1816 Torre Canavese, Domenica, b. 16

Sep 1803 Torre Canavese

    4.   Martino Tinetti, b. 28 Feb 1745 San Martino,

m. Giovanna Maria Antonia Amosso, b. abt. 1753, d. 20

Aug 1816 Torre Canavese, m2d. Maria Guglielmetti, b. abt

1758 Torre Canavese, d/o Antonio Guglielmetti and

Antonia, widow of Martini Berrutto, she d. 23 Feb 1838

Torre Canavese. Martino d. 24 Sep 1828 Torre Canavese.

All children are with Giovanna.

    vii. Maria Cattarina Tinetti, b. 24 Apr 1773 San

Martino,

    viii. Angela Domenica Tinetti, b. 3 Jul 1774, d. 11

Oct 1774 San Martino

    ix. Domenico Tinetti, b. 25 Jun 1779 San Martino, m.

Teresa Moreta, b. abt 1801, son: Antonio b. abt 1821 San

Martino, m. Domenica Pietro, b. abt 1801, d/o Pietro, m.

15 May 1850 Torre Canavese, daughter Maria Lucia, b. 3

Aug 1858 Torre Canavese

x. Giuseppe Antonio Tinetti (twin), b. 24 Aug 1780 San Martino, d. before 3 Sep 1780 San Martino, n.f.r.

xi. Angela Maria Tinetti (twin), b. 24 Aug 1780 San Martino, d. 25 Dec 1780 San Martino

xii. Giovanna Maria Tinetti, b. 4 Feb 1783 San Martino, d. 24 Jun 1855 San Martino, n.f.r.

xiii. Pietro Tinetti, b. Sep 1783 San Martino, d. 26 Aug 1784 San Martino.

xiv. Giuseppe Tinetti, b. 14 May 1784, d. 24 Jul 1784 San Martino.

xv. Antonio Tinetti, b. 1785 San Martino, n.f.r.

+xvi. Giuseppe Tinetti

xvii. Angela Domenica Tinetti, b. 5 Jul 1794 San Martino,

xviii. Martino Tinetti, b. 1800 San Martino, son: Domenico, b. 1839 Torre Canavese, m. Antonia Grosso, d/o Antonio Grosso and Maria Angela Bessola, b. abt 1835, d.9

Feb 1867 San Martino, sons: Antonio, Pietro both died in Montana.

xix. Giovanni, Tinetti b. 17 May 1804 San Martino, d. 1808 San Martino.

xx. Michele Tinetti b. abt. 1805, San Martino n.f.r.

5. Giuseppe Tinetti, b.4 Jul 1789 San Martino, m. Maria Magdalena Pastore, (see Pastore family) b. 21 Oct 1790 San Martino, d. 22 Oct 1865 Torre Canavese, Giuseppe d. 14 Feb 1860 San Giovanni dei Boschi.

xxi. Martino Tinetti, b. 20 Mar 1807 San Giovanni dei Boschi, m1, Teresa Ferrando, b. 1808 Oppido Monta, d. 10 Apr 1848 San Martino children: Antonio, b. 1836 San Giovanni, Maria, b. 2 may 1837 San Martino, Giuseppe, b. 13 May 1840 San Martino, m. Maria Teresa Tinetti (see Giovanni Tinetti family), d. before Jan. 1872 Torre Canavese, Margherita, b. 7 Nov 1832 San Martino, Angela, b. 16 Jul 1845 San Martino, m2d, Teresa Emilia Conto, children: Pietro Gioanni, b. Feb 1851 San Martino, d. 4 Nov 1855 San Martino, Lorenzo Giacomo, b. 1855 San Martino, d. 3 Jul 1857 San Martino, Pietro Secondo, b. 3 May 1858

San Martino, Benvenuto Federico, b. 18 Jul 1860 San Martino.

xxii. Antonio Giovanni Tinetti, b. 28 Sep 1808 San Giovanni dei Boschi, d. 21 Oct 1817 San Giovanni dei Boshi

xxiii. Giovanna Maria Tinetti, b. 7 May 1810 San Giovanni dei Boschi, d. 20 Jan 1833 San Giovanni dei Boschi

xxiv. Domenico Bartolomeo Tinetti, b. 3 May 1813 San Giovanni dei Boschi, m1. Marta Prieto, son, Antonio, m2. Rosa Sento, d/o Domenico Sento and Maria Mamberti, b. 1832 San Giovanni dei Boschi, m. 1 Jan 1867 San Giovanni dei Boschi, n.f.r.

xxv. Antonio Tinetti, b. 1 Sep 1816 San Giovanni dei Boschi, d. 13 Jan 1826 San Giovanni dei Boschi

xxvi. Antonio Tinetti, b.21 Jul 1818 San Giovanni dei Boschi, m. Maria Cuffaso, d/o Domenico Cuffaso and Maddalena Geosda, m. 9 Dec 1878 Torre Canavese n.f.r.

xxvii. Anna Maria Marianna Tinetti, b. 5 Jun 1821 San Giovanni dei Boschi, m. Giovanni Pricco, s/o Antonio Pricco and Margarita Marta, b. 1821, m. 19 Mar 1841 San

Giovanni dei Boschi, he d. before 1888 San Martino, she d. 5 Apr 1888 San Martino.

+xxviii. Giovanni Battista

6. Giovanni Battista Tinetti, b. 14 Jul 1825 San Giovanni dei Boschi, m1. Domenica Catterina Zanotti-Cussio d/o Secondo Zanotti and Maria Teresia Cussio, b. 11 Aug 1828 Cuceglio, m. 27 Aug 1846 San Giovanni dei Boschi, d. 3 Apr 1863 Torre Canavese.

xix. Giuseppe Ottavio Tinetti, b. 20 Nov 1846 San Giovanni dei Boschi, m. Maria b. 1860 Italy, d. 6 Apr 1906 San Francisco, California, Children: Joseph, Florindo, Augustino, Thomas, Rosie, Angelina.

xx. Antonio Amedeo Secondo Tinetti, b. 30 Mar 1849 San Giovanni dei Boschi, m. Giuseppa Basso Petrini, d/o Pietro Petrioni, m. 11 Jan 1881 Baldissero Canavese, d. before 1904, Antonio d. 27 Jan 1904 Torino. Children: Domenica Maria Teresa, Giovanni Pietro Giacomo, Dionigi Pietro Umberto.

xxi. Maria Teresa Tinetti, b.19 Jul 1852 Torre Canavese, m1. Giuseppe Tinetti, s/o Martino Tinetti and

Teresa Ferrando, b. 13 May 1840 San Martino, m. 21 Feb 1868 Torre Canavese, d. before 1872, m2. Giovanni Martino Preto, s/o Pietro Preto and Maddalena Silva, b. 1844 Torre Canavese, m. 20 Jan 1872 Torre Canavese, she d. 25 Mar 1881 Torre Canavese.

xxii. Maria Teresa Emilia Tinetti b. 16 May 1855 Torre Canavese, m. Giovanni Domenico Falletti, s/o Antonio Falletti and Maria Favero, b. 1839 Torre Canavese, m. 17 Feb 1877 Torre Canavese. (See Descendants of Maria Teresa Tinetti)

xxiii. Still born daughter, b/d. 7 Feb 1858 Torre Canavese

xxiv. Virginia Tinetti, b. 2 Jul 1859 Torre Canavese, d. 7 Feb 1883 Torre Canavese

xxv. Still born daughter, b/d. 12 Jan 1862 Torre Canavese

m2d. Maria Catterina Zanotti-Cussio d/o Secondo Secondo Zanotti and Maria Teresia Cussio, b. 26 Jan 1830 Cuceglio, m. 14 Aug 1878 Torre Canavese, d. before 1904 (See Zanotti family). He d. 11 Oct 1904.

xxvi. Giuseppe Secondo Tinetti, b. 23 Jan 1866 Torre Canavese, d. 7 Aug 1866 Torre Canavese

xxvii. Maria Teresa Rosa Tinetti (twin), b. 15 Oct 1868 Torre Canavese, m. Luigi Bonino s/o Giovanni Matteo Bonino and Maria Domenica Giustat, b. 30 Sep 1857 Pont-Canavese, m. 16 Aug 1885 Torre Canavese, d. 19 Apr 1920 Coalgate, Coal, Oklahoma, Rosa d. 9 May 1942 McAlester, Pittsburg, Oklahoma (See Descendants of Rosa Tinetti)

xxviii. Maria Teresa Domenica "Minnie" Tinetti, b. 15 Oct 1868 Torre Canavese, m. Pietro Giovanni (Peter) Peretti s/o Giovanni Battista Peretti and Maria Catterina Vironda, b. 25 Dec 1850 Priacco, m. 20 Jun 1888 Coal City, Grundy, Illinois, d. 14 Aug 1946 Coal City, Grundy, Illinois, Minnie d. 15 Apr 1946 Coal City, Grundy, Illinois. (See Descendants of Minnie Tinetti)

xxix. Maria Teresa Albina Tinetti, b. 14 Jun 1870 Torre Canavese, m. Carlo Marchello Bonatto, b. abt 1868, she d. 1944. (See Descendants of Albina Tinetti)

+xxx. Angela Margherita "Angelina" Tinetti

xxxi. Adele Secondina Maria Teresa Tinetti, b. 6 May 1877 Torre Canavese, d. 27 Dec 1880 Torre Canavese.

7. Angela Margherita "Angelina" Tinetti, b. 5 Dec 1871
    Torre Canavese, m. Frank Stefani s/o Giovanni Luigi
    Stefani and Elisabetta Maria Catterina Wegher (See
    Stefani Family)

Descendants of Maria Teresa Emilia Tinetti

m. Giovanni Domenico Falletti, s/o Antonio Falletti

and Maria Favero, b. 1839 Torre Canavese, m. 17 Feb 1877

Torre Canavese. Children:

i. Giovanni Falletti, b. 1886 Torre Canavese, wife

unk. n.f.r.

ii. Sebastiani Angelo Falletti, b. 11 Jan 1888 Torre

Canavese, m. Antonia Marianna Barello d/o Domenico

Barello and Maddalena Pricco, b. 24 Mar 1889 Torre

Canavese, m. 6 May 1910 Torre Canavese

b. Giovanni Falletti, b. abt. 1913, m. Maria Barion

aa. Eede b. abt. 1938

c. Domenico Falletti, b. abt. 1915

bb. Roberto Falletti

cc. Franco Falletti

iii. Maria Giovanna Falletti, b. 23 Jun 1890 Torre Canavese, m. Giusto Giovanni Giuseppe Testa. s/o Giovanni Testa and Giuseppa Guglielmetti, b. 16 Feb 1891 Torre Canavese

d. Antonio Testa, b. abt. 1909, m. Domenica Antonino

    dd. Fulvia Testa, b. abt. 1931

    aaa. Barbara

    bbb. Mauro

    ee. Italo Testa, b. abt. 1939, m. Denise

    e. Teresina Testa

    ff. Armando

    gg. Marco

    hh. Gian Giusto

    ii. Bruna

    ccc. Roberto

    ddd. Paolo

    eee. Marco

    fff. Mariateresa

    ggg. Giuliana

    f. Giuseppina

v. Domenica Maria Testa, b. 3 Feb 1894 Torre Canavese, m. Giuseppe Pistono,

g. Domenica Maria m. Chinota

jj. Maria Chinota

kk. Tarcisio Chinota, m. Domenica

hhh. Flora

aaaa. Simone

Descendants of Maria Teresa Rosa Tinetti and Luigi Bonino

i. Mary Bonino, b. 4 Sep 1886 Coal City, Grundy, Illinois, d. 19 Jul 1887 Coal City, Grundy, Illinois

ii. Angelina Bonino, b. 1 Jan 1888, Coal City, Grundy, Illinois, m. Jess Angelo Flor, s/o Cesere Flor and Clemintina Menghini, b. 6 Mar 1886 Arsio, Brez, Austria, d. 28 Jul 1934 Sherman, Grayson, Texas, Angelina d. 14 Nov 1912 Philips, Coal, Oklahoma.

h. Louis Jess Flor, b. 5 Jul 1910 Philips, Coal, Oklahoma, d. 12 May 1964 Coal City, Coal, Oklahoma

i. James Angelo Flor, b. 6 Nov 1912 Philips, Coal, Oklahoma, m. Effie Mary Menghini, d/o Edwino Menghini and Margaret Bettasso, b. 3 Jan 1920 Philips, Coal, Oklahoma, d. 30 Jan 2017, California, James d. 8 Feb 1998 Midwest City, Oklahoma, Oklahoma.

ll. Ruth Ann Flor, m. Joseph Bernard Marcotte, Jr.

mm. Margie Lee Flor, b. 3 Oct 1940 Philips, Coal, Oklahoma, m. Vernon Raymond Bode, 10 Oct 1959 Oklahoma City, Oklahoma, d. 23 Aug 2001 Oklahoma City, Oklahoma.

iii. Jim Bode

jjj. Lee Ann Bode

iii. Pearl E Bonino, b. 16 Jul 1889 Coal City, Grundy, Illinois, m. Albert Preto Satti, b. 29 Feb 1867 Tuscanio, Italy, m. 28 Apr 1908 Coalgate, Coal, Oklahoma, d. 5 Dec 1935 McAlester, Pittsburg, Oklahoma, Pearl d. 9 Aug 1947 McAlester, Pittsburg, Oklahoma

nn. Janice Satti, b. 29 Sep 1922, m. Charles Major Gouch, s/o Clarence L. Gough and Katharine G., b. 5 Nov 1926 McAlester, Pittsburg, Oklahoma, m. 12 Apr 1947 Pittsburg, Oklahoma, d. 4 Oct 1970 McAlester, Pittsburg, Oklahoma, Janice d. 26 Apr 2001 Norman, Cleveland, Oklahoma.

kkk. Charles Major Satti, Jr., d. Jun 2013

lll. Pearl Satti, m. Phil Corder

bbbb. Rebecca Corder

cccc. Melanie Corder

iv. Edward John Bonino, b. 17 Mar 1891 Pence,
Iron, Wisconsin, m. Clara Ghigo, d/o Bernardo "Barney"
Ghigo and Lucy, b. 14 May 1893 Coalgate, Indian Territory,
Oklahoma, m. 18 Jun 1913, Coalgate, Coal, Oklahoma, d. 7
Aug 1914 Coalgate, Coal, Oklahoma,

oo. Bernard Louis Bonino, b. 1 Aug 1914 Coalgate,
Coal, Oklahoma, m. Imogene England, d/o Eugene E.
England and Lucy Mae Forrester, b. abt 1917 Stigler,
Haskell, Oklahoma, m. 24 Apr 1946 Pittsburg, Oklahoma,
d. 1967 McAlester, Pittsburg, Oklahoma, Bernard d. Mar
1968 McAester, Pittsburg, Oklahoma.

ddd. Ashley Bonino

eee. James Bonino

fff. Eugene E. Bonino, m2d. Maytie Theresa Parrish
Witt d/o Edgar Lewis Parrish Witt and Laura Ann Sharp, b.
10 Oct 1891 Illinois, m. 6 mar 1930 Detroit, Wayne,
Michigan, d. 1964, Edward d. 30 Dec 1958.

v. Albert James Bonino, b.14 Oct 1892 Coalgate, Coal, Oklahoma, m. Helen Cecelia Douthitt, d/o James Perry Douthitt and Elizabeth McGoldrick, b. 25 Aug 1828 Guthrie, Logan, Oklahoma, m. 18 Oct 1915 Coalgate, Coal, Oklahoma, d. Nov 1979 Denver, Adams, Colorado, d. Nov 1986 Denver, Denver, Colorado

pp. Richard Edward Bonino, b. 29 Sep 1916 Coalgate, Coal, Oklahoma, d. 2 Aug 1918 Coalgate, Coal, Oklahoma

qq. William Lawrence Bonino, b. 15 Aug 1921 Coalgate, Coal, Oklahoma, d. 2 Nov 1941 Denver, Adams, Colorado

rr. David George Bonino, b. 23 Sep 1923 Coalgate, Coal, Oklahoma, m. Elizabeth Mary "Betty" Wedeking, d/o Harry L. Wedeking and Elizabeth F. Milligan, b. 4 Feb 1922 Colorado, m. 26 Aug 1961, d. 21 Aug 2012 Denver, Denver, Colorado, David d. 13 Nov 2004 Denver, Denver, Colorado

vi. Eda Tracilla Bonino, b. 21 Jul 1895 Coalgate, Coal, Oklahoma, m. William Earl Burr, s/o William John Burr and Sarah Ann Cottrell, b. 26 Apr 1890 Hoxie,

Sheridan, Kansas, m. 26 Apr 1926 Coalgate, Coal, Oklahoma, d. 30 Mar 1949 McAlester, Pittsburg, Oklahoma, Eda d. 3 Mar 1983 Oklahoma City, Oklahoma, Oklahoma.

ss. Louis Earl Burr, b. 26 Dec 1926, d. 12 Jan 1930 McAlester, Pittsburg, Oklahoma

tt. William Edward Burr, b. 20 Oct 1929, McAlester, Pittsburg, Oklahoma, m. Kathrine Lynette Burk, d/o Othie Glen Burk and Irene Anna Richards, b. 19 May 1943 Norfolk Virginia, d. May 1990 Oklahoma, William d. 8 Feb 1992.

ggg. Albert James Burr

hhh. Edward Glen Burr

vii. Louis Bonino, b. 2 Oct 1899 Coalgate, Coal, Oklahoma, d. 17 Jan 1900 Coalgate, Coal, Oklahoma

Descendants of Maria Teresa Domenica "Minnie" Tinetti and Peter Peretti

i. Katherine "Kate" Peretti, b. 25 Mar 1889 Braceville, Grundy, Illinois, m. Benjamin James Kessler, s/o Joseph Kessler and Pauline Marian, b. 23 Dec 1886 Oglesby, La Salle, Illinois, m. 18 Aug 1917 Ottawa, Illinois, d. 30 Oct 1954 Coal City, Grundy, Illinois, Kate d. 29 May 1984 Coal City, Grundy, Illinois.

a. Hildegard Kessler, b. 29 Dec 1912 Coal City, Grundy, Illinois, m. Donald Eugene Koerner s/o Henry Koerner and Genevieve McDonald, b. 23 Dec 1910 Manhattan, Will, Illinois, m. 10 Dec 1932 Coal City, Grundy, Illinois, d. 8 Aug 2004 Coal City, Grundy, Illinois

aa. Donald Benjamin Koerner, b. 7 Nov 1933 Joliet, Will, Illinois, m1. Joyce Marie Thomson, d/o Clarence James Thomson and Myrtle Marie Bumgarner, b. 21 Jan 1935 Illinois, m. 2 Apr 1956 Crown Point, Lake, Indiana, d. 27 Jun 1975 Joliet, Will, Illinois, Donald d. 20 Jul 2014 Joliet, Will, Illinois.

iii. Linda Koerner

jjj. Kim Koerner

kkk. Debbie Koerner

lll. Deanna Koerner

mmm. Terri Koerner

nnn. Mark Koerner

ooo. David Koerner

iii. Steven, Koerner

m.2. Shirley Diane Herr, d/o Floyd Glenn Herr and Constance Frances Lucenti, b. 18 Feb 1944 Tyler, Smith, Texas, m. 21 Jul 1973 Joliet, Will, Illinois, (four of the children noted above are hers, no data which), d. 31 May 2005 Winooka, Will, Illinois, Donald d. 20 Jul 2014, Joliet, Will, Illinois.

bb. Marlene Koerner, b. 31 May 1939 Joliet, Will, Illinois, m. George R. Bohac, Jr., s/o George R. Bohac and Florence, b. 18 Jul 1939 Braidwood, Will, Illinois, m. 21 May 1959, d. 17 Sep 1971 Joliet, Will, Illinois, Marlene d. unk. Braidwood, Will, Illinois. m2d. Daniel Joseph Cromp, s/o Edwin Cromp and Annie May Wardas, b. 26 Feb 1946 Cook,

St. Louis, Minnesota, m. 29 Apr 1967, d. 18 Feb 2011 Braidwood, Will, Illinois.

jjj. Dan, Bohac, Jr.

kkk. Jeffrey Bohac

lll. Lynn Bohac, m. Pampuch

mmm. Amy Bohac, m. Henson

cc. Katharine Louise "Kay" Koerner, b. 4 Jan 1918 Coal City, Coal, Illinois, m. Satimo "Sam" Gualandi s/o Bartolomeo Adelmo "Delmo" Gualandi and Angiolina Bernabei, b. 29 Oct 1918 Dalzell, Bureau, Illinois, m. 12 Jun 1965, d. 18 Jul 1999 Coal City, Grundy, Illinois, Kay d. 5 Jul 2006 Coal City, Grundy, Illinois.

dd. Benjamin Charles Koerner, b. 1 Oct 1919 Coal City, Coal, Illinois, m. Josephine Ione McElroy, d/o Alexander John McElroy and Annie S. McNamara, b. 12 Oct 1922 Braidwood, Will, Illinois m. 26 Apr 1941 Braidwood, Will, Illinois, d. 18 Nov 2008 Laveen, Maricopa, Arizona, Benjamin d. 23 Mar 2003 Sun City West, Maricopa, Arizona

nnn. Ben Leroy Koerner, m. Marybell Lightseg, n.f.r.

ooo. Madonna Rae, m. Charles Hart, s/o Carlton Wells Hart, Jr. and Donnamae Gaunt (Sanford), n.f.r.

aaaa. Christine

ii. John Albert Peretti, b. 11 Jul 1890, Braceville, Grundy, Illinois, d. 18 Mar 1949, Coal City, Grundy, Illinois, n.f.r.

iii. Peter Peretti, Jr., b. 15 Apr 1893, Braceville, Grundy, Illinois, d. 5 Sep 1981 Cook County, Illinois, fought in WW I, n.f.r.

iv. Charles Guido Peretti, b. 29 Oct 1894 Braceville, Grundy, Illinois, d. 14 Oct 1953 Coal City, Grundy, Illinois, fought in WWI, n.f.r.

v. James Romeo Peretti, b. 23 May 1896 Braceville, Grundy, Illinois, m. Catherine "Kate" Gruber, d/o George August Gruber and Annie Schett, b. 1 Jan 1917 Chicago, Cook, Illinois, m. 27 Aug 1921 Coal City, Grundy, Illinois, d. May 1972, Chicago, Cook, Illinois

a. James Edward Peretti, b. 30 Sep 1924, Chicago, Cook, Illinois, d. 18 Jun 2006 Lancaster, Los Angeles, California, n.f.r.

b. Robert Charles Peretti, b. 3 Dec 1927, Chicago, Cook, Illinois, m. Betty Jean Duncan, d/o Joseph W. and Mayme Duncan, b. 3 Apr 1935 Fosters, Tuscaloosa, Alabama, m. 17 Apr 1954 Chicago, Cook, Illinois, d. 8 Feb 2009, Burbank, Cook, Illinois, Robert d. 30 Dec 2001, Burbank, Cook, Illinois.

aa. Renee Jean Peretti, b. 4 Jan 1956, Chicago, Cook, Illinois, d. 30 Sep 1975, Olmstad Co., Minnesota, n.f.r.

bb. Robert Charles Peretti, b. 11 Mar 1957, Evergreen Park, Cook, Illinois, d. 23 Sep 1981, Cook, Illinois, in Air Force 977-1980, n.f.r.

c. Arthur Peretti, b. 19 Aug 1933, Cook, Illinois, m. Barbra Dyer, m. 5 Jun 1957, Cook, Illinois, n.f.r.

d. Ronald George Peretti, b. 2 Jan 1936, Ilinois, m. Beverly Sue Howell, d/o Lloyd Ferald Howell and Mary Evadine Alvis, b. 13 Aug 1939. Fort Benjamin Harrison,

Marion, Indiana, m. 28 Oct 1957, Cook, Illinois, d. 2 Feb 2011, North Judson, Starke, Indiana, Ronald d. 1 Oct 2016 North Judson, Starke, Indiana

cc. Ronald George Peretti, Jr., m. Deloris Deiane Wasily, d/o Anthony Wasily and Alvera Caposey.

aaa. Kimberly Marie Peretti, m1 Lee Eric Patterson, m2 Michael l. Back, n.f.r.

bbb. Ronald George Peretti, III, b. 10 May 1980, Munster, Lake, Indiana, m. Michelle Lynn Gerhart, d/o Michael Tad Gerhart and Donna Kaye Minix, Ronald d. 22 Feb 2011, Winmac, Pulaski, Indiana

aaaa. Caloe Peretti

dd. James R. Peretti, m. Carol S. Brunke, d/o Walter Emmett Brunke and Virginia Mae Bryson, n.f.r.

William Anthony Peretti, m. Teresa Jean Noble, d/o Gene Noble and Roseann Evelyn Romenzak, b. 5 jan 1967 Knox, Starke, Indiana, d. 23 Sep 1994 Knox, Starke, Indiana, m2 Allafair Prater, d/o Loss Prater and Flossie A. Howard.

ff. John Michael Peretti, Sr. b. abt 1978, Illinois, m1, Sherry M. Wireman, d/o Jesse Wireman and Judith Audrey Smith, m2, Andrea Yvonne Wireman, d/o Ernst Rodeny Wireman and Vonda Gay Prater, m3, Christina Romans, n.f.r.

ccc. John Michael Peretti, Jr. n.f.r.

gg. Eugene Leroy Peretti, b. 16 Aug 1938 Illinois, m. Judith Ann Hickey, d/o Harold and Regina Hickey, b. 19 Oct 1940, m. 28 Mar 1958 Cook, Illinois, d. 22 May 2013, Romeoville, Will, Illinois, Eugene d. 3 Nov 2015 Romeoville, Will, Illinois.

ddd. Eugene Peretti, b. abt 1960

bbbb. Holly Peretti, m. Michael Ricca

aaaaa. Ceyde Ricca n.f.r.

bbbbb. Rikki Ricca, n.f.r.

cccc. Becky Peretti, n.f.r.

eee. Pamela M. Peretti, n.f.r.

hh. Jackie Peretti, b. abt 1940 n.f.r.

ii. Jerry Peretti, b. abt 1942 n.f.r.

vi. Florence Peretti, b. 23 May 1896 Braceville, Grundy, Illinois, d. 6 Jun 1896 Braceville, Grundy, Illinois

vii. Jessie Marie Peretti, b. 17 Sep 1898 Braceville, Grundy, Illinois, m. Edward James Bubnar, s/o John Bubnar and Anna Sotak, b. 14 Nov 1892, Mohanna Plains, Pennsylvania, m. 12 May 1917 Illinois, d. 25 Jun 1977, Port Hueneme, Ventura, California, Jessie d. 15 Feb 1971 Libertyville, Lake, Illinois.

jj. Ina Jessie Bubnar, b.14 Mar 1918, Chicago, Cook, Illinois, m1. John Emright Harkness, s/o James Harkness and Winifred Emright, b. 5 May 1901 Illinois, m. 14 Jan 1939 Sterling, Whiteside, Illinois, d. 5 Jul 1941 Elgin, Kane, Illinois, m2, Harry B. Ellis, s/o Clarence M. Ellis and Tessa Boardman, b. 12 Sep 1907 Cairo, Alexander, Illinois, d. 29 Oct 1977 Vero Beach, Indian River, Florida, Ina d. 23 Mar 1979 Oxnard, Ventura, California.

viii. Ina Mable Bubnar, b. 6 Apr 1920 Chicago, Cook, Illinois, m. Sydney Henry Madderom, s/o John C.

Madderom and Effie Wyma, b. 8 Mar 1919 Chicago, Cook, Illinois, m. 6 Feb 1939 Newton, Indiana, d. 7 Jan 1999, Hayward, Alameda, California, Irene d. 10 Sep 2001. Hayward, Alameda, California

kk. Douglas John Madderom, m. Marcia Van Proyen, n.f.r.

ll. Judith Ann Madderom, m. Ronald C. Churchill, n.f.r.

ix. Pearl Edna Bubnar, b. 3 Feb 1922, Chicago, Cook, Illinois, m. Orville Clair Brogan, s/o James William Brogan and Margaret Giblin, Pearl d. 23 Feb 1991 Carson City, Carson, Nevada

mm. Daniel Clair Brogan, b. 20 Sep Chicago, Cook, Illinois, m. Lorraine Gayle Cape, Daniel d. 21 Jul 2013, n.f.r.

nn. Janice L. Brogan, m. Gary Robert Morin, n.f.r.

oo. Curtis O. Brogan, m. Kimberly A. Curtis, n.f.r.

pp. Ronda J. Brogan, m. Frederic Leland Smith, n.f.r.

qq. Lynette Brogan, n.f.r.

rr. Denise Brogan, m. Whitford n.f.r.

ss. Norine L Brogan, m. Tan F. Faircloth, n.f.r.

tt. James Brogan, n.f.r.

x. Edward John Bubnar, b. 16 Nov 1923 Chicago, Cook, Illinois, m. Clara Lee Knowlton, d/o Arthur Daniel Knowlton and Lena Irene Martin, b. 31 Jan 1926 Sheridan, Wyoming, d. 17 Feb 2018 California, Edward d. 17 Jul 2004 Oxnard, Ventura, California

uu. Dennis Clair Bubnar, m. Susan Jacqueline Bates, d/o Franklin Lawton Bates and Betty Louise Gibson, b. 17 May 1949 Bexar, Texas, d. 5 May 2012 California, Dennis d. 5 May 2012 Oxnard, Ventura, California

fff. Lori B. Bubnar, m.Tim Jackson, n.f.r.

dddd. Caleb Jackson, n.f.r.

ggg. Tyson E. Bubnar, m. Terri, n.f.r.

eeee. Bailey Bubnar, n.f.r.

ffff. Juliette Bubnar, n.f.r.

gggg. Isabelle, n.f.r.

hhhh. Matthew, n.f.r.

iiii. Megan, n.f.r.

vv. Lynda Lee Bubnar, m. James D. Cox, m2 Mike Fitzhugh,

xi. Betty Jane Cox, b. 16 Nov 1925 Chicago, Cook, Illinois, d. 27 Aug 1931 Chicago, Cook, Illinois

viii. Edith Peretti, b. 2 Dec 1899 Braceville, Grundy, Illinois, m. John Edward Bubnar, s/o John Bubnar and Susanna Dobas, b. 8 Jul 1897 Pottsville, Schuykill, Pennsylvania, m. 21 Sep 1920 Chicago, Cook, Illinois, d. 7 Jun 1965 Spokane, Spokane, Washington, Edith d. 27 Mar 1926 Detroit, Wayne, Michigan

ww. John Robert Bubnar, b. 24 Jul 1921 Chicago, Cook, Illinois, m1 Helen Ruth Leman/Leman, d/o Edwin Lionel Leman and Mary Luvina Stuck, b. 28 Oct 1922 Nemo, Lawrence, South Dakota, div. 3 may 1945 Olympia, Thurston, Washington, m2 Jane Elizabeth Medrow, d/o Arthur Medrow and Beatrice Ester John, b. 7 Dec 1917

Milwaukee, Milwaukee, Wisconsin, m. 26 Dec 1962 Nevada, div 29 Aug 1983 Fontana, San Bernadino, California, d. 24 Feb 2001 Fontana, San Bernardino, California, m3 Gertrude A. Baker, m. 19 Mar 1985 Reno, Washoe, Nevada, John d. 5 Sep 2011 Rialto, San Bernardino, California

xx. Lorraine Bubnar, b. 19 Feb 1925 Chicago, Cook, Illinois, m1 Bise, m2 Buford Cecil Little, Jr., s/o Buford Cecil Little and Lola Mae Harrison, b. 24 Jun 1927 Jackson, Hinds, Mississippi, m. 4 Nov 1956 Clark, Nevada, d. 10 Nov 2010 Florence, Rankin, Mississippi, WW II Vet

hhh. Suzanne Little, m. Ted Derrick, n.f.r.

iii. Sandra Little, m. Thomas Fortenberry

jjj. Ronald Buford Little, m. Terry Lynn Smith, n.f.r.

kkk. Edward M. Little, m. Laura

xxi. Irma Bubnar, b. abt. 1929 Chicago, Cook, Illinois, d. abt. 1929 Chicago, Cook, Illinois

vii. Minnie Theresa Peretti, b. 14 Jun 1903 Braceville, Grundy, Illinois, m1. John Francis Smith, b. 4 Oct 1898

Marine City, St. Clair, Michigan, m. 1 Aug 1921 Cook, Illinois, d. bef. 1934

xxii. Delores Frances Smith, b. 8 Nov 1922, Mt. Greenwood, Chicago, Cook, Illinois, m. Wallace Herbert McClain, s/o Walter Simms Hugh McClain and Alice Caroline Jones, b. 30 Oct 1896 Hardin, Marshall, Kentucky, m2 26 May 1958, d. 25 Sep 1974 Benton, Marshall, Kentucky

xxiii. John J. Smith, b. 7 Sep 1924 Mt. Greenwood, Chicago, Cook, Illinois, m. June Vinson 11 Sep 1954 Chicago, Cook, Illinois, John J. d. 28 May 1991 Merrillville, Lake, Indiana

lll. Barbara Ann Smith, m. Austin Loren Lewis, n.f.r.

mmm. Allison L. Smith, m. Johnson n.f.r.

Minnie Theresa m2. Julius Nicolaus Benning, s/o Peter Frederik Benning and Karna Nilsdotter, b. 5 Mar 1889 Fredericksberg, Copenhaven, Denmark, m. 9 Jul 1934 Cook, Illinois, d. 29 Jul 1953 Chicago, Cook, Illinois, Minnie d. 15 Oct 1989 Cook, Illinois nn. Julius Gerald Benning, b. 9 Oct 1935 Chicago, Cook, Illinois, m. Gloria June Ebeling, d/o John A. Ebeling and Josephine G. Boza, b. 3 Jan 1938 Blue Island, Cook, Illinois, m. 15 Jul 1961 Illinois, d. 15 Jun 1997 New Lenox, Will, Illinois, Julius d. 15 Jan 1991 Illinois

jjj. Keith James, n.f.r.

oo. Richard Charles Benning, m. Mary Lou Bale, m2 Linda S. Pence

(Children with Mary Lou Bale

kkk. Peggy Sue Benning, n.f.r.

ll. Melissa Elaine Benning, n.f.r.

mm. Robert Michael Benning, n.f.r.

pp. Karen A. Benning, m. Gerald Lavalle, n.f.r.

viii. Louis V. Peretti, b. 26 Jan 1906 Braceville, Grundy, Illinois, m. Catherine "Kay" Byrnes, d/o John Byrnes and Mary Kane, m. 5 Jun 1927 Chicago, Cook, Illinois, div. bef. 1940, Louis d. 28 Aug 1992 Coal City, Grundy, Illinois

xxiv. Louis Andrew Perreth, b.

1 Dec 1929 Chicago, Cook, Illinois, m. Barbara Jean McDermott, d/o William McDermott and Grace, b. 7 Sep 1930 Wisconsin, Louis d. 21 Oct 1996 Green Bay, Brown, Wisconsin, n.f.r.

ix. Alma Elizabeth Peretti, b. 26 Aug 1908 Braceville, Grundy, Illinois, m. Arthur William Jackson, s/o Frank L. Jackson and Chloe Prine, b. 17 Oct 1908 Peru, Miami, Indiana, m. 21 Dec 1932 Chicago, Cook, Illinois, d. 22 Jan 1986 Clearwater, Pinellas, Florida, Alma d. 28 Mar 1985 Koontz Lake, Marshall, Indiana

xxv. Lois Ruth Jackson, b. 30 Dec 1936 Chicago, Cook, Illinois, m. Michael Guilfoyle, b. 24 Jul 1928, m. 6 Nov 1954 Chicago, Cook, Illinois, d. 5 Jun 2008 Hometown, Cook, Illinois, n.f.r.

xxvi. Frank William Jackson, m. Ellen J. Degani, d/o Michael L, Degani and Pauline Whittenburg, n.f.r.

xxvii. Arthur C. Jackson, m. Betty n.f.r.

xxviii. Albert L. Jackson, b. 5 Jan 1945 Chicago, Cook, Illinois, m. Jeanene L. Brooks, b. 21 Nov 1942, m. 5 Mar 1966 Chicago, Cook, Illinois, Albert d. 30 Apr 2008 St Petersburg, Pinellas, Florida

xxix. Diane Jackson, m. Frank Dellachiale, n.f.r.

qq. Brian Arthur Dellachiale, m. Shannon Marie Valliere,

Descendants of Maria Teresa Albina Tinetti and Carlo Marchello Bonatto

1. Domenica Bonatto, b. 1900 Torino (Turin), Torino, Italy, m. Luigi Coltro, b. abt 1900, Domenica d. 1972 Torino, Torino, Italy
   a. Giovanni Coltro, b. 1930, Torino, Torino, Italy, d. 2006 Torino, Torino, Italy
   b. Maria Rosa Colto (twin), b. 12 Oct 1933 Torino, Torino, Italy, d. 1984 Torino, Torino, Italy
   c. Marco Coltro (twin), b. 12 Oct 1933 Torino, Torino, Italy, m. Maria Teresa Reineri, b. abt 1935
   aa. Luca

   aaa. Camilla Coltro, b. Abt. 2002

2. Teresina Bonatto, m. (uk. First name) Da
   a. Paolo
3. Severino Bonatto, m. Palmera Alarasti
   a. Teresa Bonatto, m. Arena Dose
aa. Paola Bonatto

   b. Anna Maria Bonatto, n.f.r.
4. Caterina Bonatto, m. Luigi Malvassora, d. 1964 Italy
   c. Elsa Malvassora
   d. Piercarlo Malvassora

The Pastore Family of San Martino

The name Pastore means "shepherd." It is found throughout Italy.

1. Antonino Pastore, b. abt 1694, m. Lucia, n.f.r.
2. Pietro Antonio Pastore, b. 14 Aug 1719 San Martino, Torino, Italy, m. Maria Guicidati, b. abt 1725 n.f.r.
3. Domenico Matteo Antonio Pastore, b. 21 Feb 1745 San Martino, Torino, Itlay, m. Maria Martinetto, d/o Antonio Martinetto, d. 27 Nov 1786 San Martino, Torino
4. Bartolomeo, b. 8 Nov 1753 San Martino, m. Giovanna Motto, d/o Giuseppe Motto and Marta, b. abt 1767 San Martino, Torino, Italy, m. 6 Oct 1781

San Martino, Torino, Italy, Bartolomeo d. 7 Jul 1837
San Martino, Torino, Italy

a. Margherita, b. 27 Mar 1788 San Martino, Torino, Italy, d. 8 Oct 1856 San Martino, Torino, Italy

b. +Maria Magdalena

c. Catterina, b. 26 Jun 1792 San Martino, Torino, Italy, d. bef 1794

d. Catterina, b.17 May 1794 San Martino, Torino, Italy, M. Giovanni Frej, s/o Giuseppe Frej, b. 23 Feb 1791 San Martino, orino, Italy, d. 17 May 1842 San Martino, Torino, Italy, Catterina d. 29 Jun 1841 San Martino, Torino, Italy

e. Domenica, b. 13 Apr 1795 San Martino. Torino, Italy, m. Antonio Bellardi, b. 14 Jan 1797 Strambino, Torino, Italy d. 21 Jul 1867 San Martino, Torino, Italy Domenica d. 27 Jan 1852 San Martino, Torino, Italy

f. Marta, b. 25 Jan 1800 San Martino, Torino, Italy, m1. Antonio Sissoldo-Carlin, b. 27 May 1807 San Martino, Torino, Italy, d. 26 Feb San Martino, Torino, Italy, m2 Francesco Marta, b. 11 Jul 1807 San Martino, Torino, Italy, d. 18 Aug 1870, Marta d. 10 Jul 1867 San Martino, Torino, Italy

g. Giuliana, b. 31 Jul 1805 San Martino, Torino, Italy, m. Lorenzo Marta, s/o Battista Marta and

Domenica Andrina, b. 29 Mar 1795 San
Martino, Torino, Italy, Giuliana d. 28 Jun 1864
San Martino, Torino, Italy

5. Maria Magdalena Pastore, b. 21 Oct 1790, m.
Giuseppe Tinetti (See the Tinetti Family)

The Motto Family

Motto comes from Motta, a Gaulish word meaning hill.

1. Giuseppe Motto, b. abt 1700 n.f.r.
2. Martino Motto, b. abt 1728, m. Martha, n.f.r.
3. Giuseppe Motto, b. 21 Sep 1753 San Martino,
   Torino, Italy, m. Marta, b. abt 1737, d. 15 Apr 1807
   San Martino, Torino, Italy, Giuseppe d. before his
   wife.
4. Giovanna Motto (see Tinetti Family)

The Zanotti Family

The name Zanotti basically means "Little John",
Zani is a variation of John that was popular from the 14th
Century. The name is found throughout Italy, most
prominently in the Lombardia, Emilia-Romagna and
Piedmont regions.

1. Domenico Zanotti, b. abt 1638, n.f.r.
2. Francesco Zanotti, b. abt. 1663, n.f.r.
3. Pietro Zanotti, b. abt. 1688 Cuceglio, Torino, Italy n.f.r.
4. Bartolomeo Zanotti, b. abt. 1713, m. Cattarina Genta, b. abt 1718 n.f.r.
5. Eusebio Zanotti, b. abt 1738 Cuceglio, Torino, Italy, m. Francesca Bezutti, d/o Carlo Bezutti and Margherita Pezzi, b. abt 1744 Cuceglio, Torino, Italy, d. 5 Jan 1826 Cuceglio, Torino, Italy
    +a.Carlo Bartolomeo

    b. Bartolomeo, b. 9 Oct 1766 Cuceglio, Torino, Italy n.f.r.
    c. Battista, b. 13 Jan 1767 Cuceglio, Torino, Italy n.f.r.
    d. Maria Margherita, b. 13 Mar 1769 Cuceglio, Torino, Italy n.f.r.
    e. Giovanni Antonio, b. 20 Jan 1770 Cuceglio, Torino, Italy n.f.r.
6. Carlo Zanotti, b. 8 Apr 1764 Cuceglio, Torino, Italy, m. Domenica Pastore, d/o Simon Pastore and Cattarina (see Pastore family of Cuceglio), b. 7 Aug 1753 Cuceglio, Torino, Italy, m. 15 Jan 1785 Cuceglio, Torino, Italy, Carlo d. Dec 1809 Cuceglio, Torino, Italy
    b. Antonio, b. 17 Sep 1784 Cuceglio, Torino, Italy,

c. Francesca, b. 13 Nov 1785 Cuceglio, Torino, Italy,

d. Margherita Maria, b. 19 Feb 1788 Cuceglio, Torino, Italy, n.f.r.

e. Eusebio Giovanni, b. 17 Jul 1790 Cuceglio, Torino, Italy, n.f.r.

f. Cattarina, b. 27 Feb 1792 Cuceglio, Torino, Italy,

g. Maria Cattarina, b. 7 Jun 1794 Cuceglio, Torino, Italy, n.f.r.

h. Simon, b. 27 Apr 1796 Cuceglio, Torino, Italy,

i. Giuseppe, b. abt 1798 Cuceglio, Torino, Italy, n.f.r.

j. Antonio, b. abt 1799 Cuceglio, Torino, Italy, m. Celesta Cussio, d/o Giacomo Antonio Cussio and Maria Cattarina Henrico (see Cussion Family), b. abt 1810, m. 9 Feb 1828 Cuceglio, Torino, Italy, Antonio d. 11 Jul 1877 Cuceglio, Torino, Italy

aa. Giovanna Domenica Lucia, b. 27 Dec 1834 Cuceglio, Torino, Italy, m. Giuseppe Cussio, b. abt 1840

bb. Maria Lissia, b. 20 Nov 1835 Cuceglio, Torino, Italy, n.f.r.

cc. Maria Teresa, b. 30 Jul 1838 Cuceglio, Torino, Italy, n.f.r.

dd. Giovanni Antonio, b. 19 Oct 1840 Cuceglio, Torino, Italy, n.f.r.

ee. Carlo Antonio, b. 1840 Cuceglio, Torino, Italy,

7. Secondo Zanotti, b. abt 1803 Cuceglio, Torino, Italy, m. Maria Teresia Cussio, d/o Giacomo Antonio Cussio and Maria Cattarino Henrico, b. 7 May 1807 Cuceglio, Torino, Italy, m. 9 Feb 1828 Cuceglio, Torino, Italy, d. bef. 1846 Cuceglio, Torino, Italy, Secondo d. 31 dec 1838 Cuceglio, Torino, Italy

+o. Domenica Cattarina

p. Carlo Antonio, b. 15 Dec 1829 Cuceglio, Torino, Italy n.f.r.

+q. Maria Cattarina

r. Carlo Antonio, b. 4 May 1833 Cuceglio, Torino, Italy n.f.r.

Celesta Maria, b. 6 Nov 1834 Cuceglio, Torino, Italy

t. Clara Rosa, b. 10 Nov 1836, Cuceglio, Torino, Italy

8. Domenica Cattarina, b. 11 Aug 1828 Cuceglio, Torino, Italy, m. Giovanni Tinetti (see Tinetti Family)

9. Maria Catterina, b. 26 Jan 1830 Cuceglio, Torino, Italy, m. Giovanni Tinetti (see Tinetti family)

The Bezutti Family

I couldn't find any data on the name Bezutti.

1. Antonio Bezutti, b. abt. 1668 n.f.r.
2. Giuseppe Bezutti, b. abt. 1693 n.f.r.
3. Carlo Bezutti, b. abt. 1718 Cuceglio, Torino, Italy, m. Margarita Pezzi, b. abt. 1723 Cuceglio, Torino, Italy, n.f.r.
4. Francesca Bezutti, b. abt. 1744 Cuceglio, Torino, Italy, m. Eusebio Zanotti (see Zanotti family), d. 5 Jan 1826 Cuceglio, Torino, Italy

The Pastore Family of Cuceglio

1. Eusebio Pastore, b. abt 1700, m. Magdalena, b. abt 1705

2. Simon Pastore, b. 2 Mar 1725 Cuceglio, Torino, Italy, m. Cattarina, b. abt 1730, n.f.r.
3. Domenica Pastore, b. 7 Aug 1753 Cuceglio, Torino, Italy, m. Carlo Zanotti (see Zanotti Family)

The Cussio Family

The meaning of this name is unknown but it is a Latin of Germanic origins, "Cussa" or "Kussa." It is often written with the long "s" which looks like an "f" so it has been misinterpreted as "Cuffia." Since Angelina told her children and granddaughters that the name was "Cussio" that is how I have recorded it.

1. Martino Cussio, b. abt. 1712, n.f.r.
2. Pietro Antonio Cussio, b. abt. 1737, m. Lucia Rossino, b. abt. 1742, n.f.r.
3. Augusto Martino, b. 13 Aug 1762 Cuceglio, Torino, Italy, m. Maria Zanotti, d/o Domenico Zanotti, b. abt 1758, n.f.r.
4. Giacomo Antonio Cussio, b. 15 Feb 1778 Cuceglio, Torino, Italy, m1., Maria Catterina Henrico, d/o Dominco Henrico and Maria Berutti, b. 7 Mar 1779 Cuceglio, Torino, Italy, m. abt 1801, d. bef. 1810,

a. Maria Rosa, b. 11 Feb 1802 Cuceglio, Torino, Italy n.f.r.

b. Rosa, b. 11 Aug 1804 Cuceglio, Torino, Italy n.f.r.

c. Antonio, b. 1 Jun 1806 Cuceglio, Torino, Italy n.f.r.

+d. Maria Teresia

d. Celesta (Celestina), b. abt. 1810 Cuceglio, Torino, Italy, m. Antonio Zanotti, (see Zanotti Family)

Giacomo m2 Helena Magdalena Fantino, d/o Domenico Fantino, widow of Andreas Curso, m. 30 Apr 1810 Cuceglio, Torino, Italy,

Maria Margherita, b. 29 Jan 1812 Cuceglio, Torino, Italy, n.f.r.

Maria Teresia Cussio, b. 7 May 1807 Cuceglio, Torino, Italy, m. Secondo Zanotti (see Zanotti Family)

The Henrico/Enrico Family

This is the name "Henry." The Italian version is Enrico. It is spelled in the records both ways interchangeably.

Pietro Henrico, b. abt. 1725 n.f.r.

Domenico Henrico, b. abt. 1754 Cuceglio, Torino, Italy, m. Maria Berutto, b. abt. 1759 Cuceglio, Torino, Italy, n.f.r.

Maria Cattarina, b. 7 Mar 1779 Cuceglio, Torino, Italy, m. Giacomo Antonio Cussio (see Cussio Family) d. bef. 1810

Selective Bibliography

1. Bertolini, Fabio, Belli, William e Rusconi, Tiziana, Sporminore, Segni e Memorie, Arti Grafiche Saturnia, Trento 2000

2. Bolognani, Bonifacio, A Courageous People from the Dolomites, Typolithography T.E.M I, Trento 1981

3. Brunelli, Louis, Filo Magazine, New York. Filo.tiroles.com

4. Chiesa Cattolica, Salt City , Utah: filmato dalla Genealogical Society of Utah

   1988 Parrochia di San Giovanni (Torino) film/DGS 156341 item 2-4

   1988 Parrochia di San Martino Canavese (Torino) film/DGS 1603623, 1603624, 1603625

   1987 Parrochia di Torre Canavese (Torino) film/DGS 1518379, 15183801986 Parrochia di Sporminore (Trento) film/DGS 1388952

5. Delaney, Frank, The Celts. Little Brown and Co. Boston Toronto 1986

6. Fucilla, Joseph G., Our Italian Surnames, Baltimore: Genealogical Publishing Co., Inc.

7. Gould, Virginia, Information on his father while reminiscing with Clement Stefani, unpublished manuscript 28 Jun 1977, copy in possession of Wendy Negley, Beaverton, Oregon

8. Gould, Virginia, Reminiscing with Aunt Dell, unpublished manuscript, ca. 1970, copy in possession of Wendy Negley, Beaverton, Oregon

9. Hampton, Marian, Frank Sefani's Last Days, unpublished manuscript, copy in possession of Wendy Negley, Beaverton, Oregon

10. Issaquah Historical Society, Images of America Issaquah Washington, Arcadia Publishing, Chicago, Illinois, 2002

11. Italia, Trento, Diocesi di Trento, Registri Parrochiali 1548-1937. Database with images, Family Search.org

12. McDonald, Margaret, Memories of Stefani Grandparents, unpublished manuscript ca. 1978, copy in possession of Wendy Negley, Beaverton, Oregon

13. McDonald, Margaret, Notes Concerning Frank Stefani's Early Life as told by his son, Clement, unpublished manuscript ca. 1978, copy in possession of Wendy Negley, Beaverton, Oregon

14. Micheli, Pietro, Sulle Sponde Dello Sporeggio, Trento, 1977

15. Rauzi, Gian Maria, The Face of Trento Over the Centuries, Curcu & Genovese, Trento, Italy, 2nd edition Feb. 2010

16. Smith, Michael Stephen, The Emergence of Modern Business Enterprise in France 1800-1930, Harvard University Press, 20

Subject Index

A

Adelina, name 166

Agostino, Mario 228

America 77-79, 82, 7. 98 167, 168, 177, 187, 212,223

Anauni, 25-27

C

Canavese, 147-150

Comox, B.C., 97

Cards, playing, 42, 47, 135

Castle Garden, 76 (picture) 81

Council of Trent, 32

Cuceglio, 161, 219

Cussio, name, 166

D

Dolomite Mts, Dolomiti, 19-21

Brenta Dolomites 20

Cima Tosa 20, 24

E

Education, 45-46

Englewood see Issaquah

F

Family names, data

Bezutti, 333

Conci, 285

Cussio, 166, 334

Facchini, 287

Franchetti, 281

Fridle, 288

Henrico, Enrico, 336

Magnani, 284

Melchiori, 283

Motto, 328

Olmar/Volmar, 278

Pastore 326 333

Remondini 53, 275

Stefani 249

Tinetti 295

Wegher 55 271

Zanotti 329

Filo, 41-42

Food, 38-45

    Canerdelli 43

    Gnocchi 43

    Polenta 42-45, 47

    Tortei delle patate 43-44

G

Gilman, see Issaquah

H

House 54, 50 (picture)
      52-53, 228

I

Issaquah, 98

M

Maso Milano 55, 225-227

Michigan, 82-86

    Iron mines, 86

    Iron miners, 84 picture)

Iron Mountain, 86, 237

    Norway, 86

    Pence, 224-225

    Upper Peninsula, 82

Monaco, 155-156

Monica, 16 79 87 88 206-207

Monti Palladi, see

      Dolomite Mts.

N

Napoleon Bonaparte, 51-52

Noce, 37

Nones, 27

O

Orzetto, 39

P

Pence, 238-239

Polenta, 42, 47

R

Red hair, 227

Religion, 45

Remondini family, 53

Romans, 25, 27, 148

S

Salassi, 148-150

Saloon, 103 108

San Giovanna, 161-162 219

San Martino Canavese, 154 219

Singing, 42 47

Social Security, 203

Spor Castle, 206

Sporeggio, 37

Spormaggiore, 31-32

Sporminore, 31-32

    Church, 224

    Description, 223

    History, 37

    Life in, 37-47

    Marriage customs, 40-41 52

    Mayor, 227

Statue of Liberty, 15, 82

Stefani family, 31-32

    Name meaning, 31

Stefani, Frank

    And father 57-58, 63-65

    And Monica, 16, 79, 87, 206-207

    Birth, 57

    Early life, 63-66

    Education, 66-68

    Report card 62 (picture)

    50th Anniversary, 141-142

    Garden, 109-110

    Emigration reasons, 77-79

    Leaving Church, 105-108

    Marriage, 89, 169

    Memory of, 133-137

    Saloon, 103, 108

    Social Security, 203

    Trip to Alaska, 175

    Work in Paris, 69-71

T

Tinetti, Angelina, 89 124-129

    Birth, 156

    Childhood, 169-170

    Death, 195

    Letters, 196-198

    Marriage, 89 169

    Midwife, 176

    Social Security, 203

    Speaking Italian, 177

    Wedding Anniversary, 141-142

Tinetti, Giovanni, 159

    160(pic)161-171, 300

    Guiseppe, 155-156, 298

    Martino, 154-155 296

Torino (Turin), 219

Torre Canavese, 154 219

Trento/Trent, 32-33 80

    Location (map), 30

    Rulers, 33

V

Val di Non, 20, 25

Vallia, 162, 220

W

Wegher family, 55

    Name, 271

Werra, 14 16 (picture)

Wisconsin

    Hurley, 86, 163, 237-238

    Pence, 238-239

Z

Zanotti, name, 165-16

Name Index

Women are listed under both their married and their maiden names. When the woman's maiden name is unknown, she is listed under her first name with the last name of her husband in parentheses. If a man's last name is known but not his first, the last name is listed with the maiden-name of his wife in parentheses. For names with various spellings such as Stefani (di Stefani, de Stefani, di Stefanis etc.) I have used the most common version of the name and put all the others under it (i.e. Stefani)

A

Adams

Adams, Andrea 263

Adams, David Alan 263

    Harold Lewis 264

    John Burr 116, 261

    Judy 262

    Julie K 263

    Harmony M.

    (Durkee) 263

    Michael L. 264

    Patricia 262

    Paul Lewis 262

    Rebecca Lynn

    ((Nichols) 263

    Richard Todd 263

    Samuel John 263

    Stephen Todd 263

Alarasti, Palmera (Bonatto) 325

Alvis, Mary Evadne

    (Howell) 314

Ammerman, Arthur

    Edward 259

    Bertha Ellen (Long) 259

    Lawrence Edward 259

    Sandra Gay 260

Amosso, Giovanna Antonia

    Marie 140 283

Anderson. Carl Olaf 26

Andrea (Adams) 263

Andrina, Domenica (Marta) 328

Angeli, Anna Domenica

    (Conci) 286

Anna (Graziani) 284

Anna (Tinetti) 295

Antonia (Guglielmetti) 296

Azario, Peter Canavese 147-148

B

Back, Michael L. 314

Baker, Gertrude A.

    (Bubnar) 320

Bale, Mary Lou (Benning) 322

Barbara (Magnani) 285

Bates, Susan Jacqueline

    (Bubnar) 319

Bellardi, Antonio 327

Benson, Bertha Ann 259

Benning, Gloria June

(Ebeling) 322

Gerald 322

Julius Nicolaus 322

Karen A (Lavalle) 323

Keith James 322

Mary Lou (Bale)

Melissa Elaine 323

Peggy Sue 323

Peter Frederick 322

Richard Julius Charles 323

Robert Michael 323

Bergsma, Pietje (Peechie)

    (Stefani) 266

Henry Tjeerd 266

Berotto, Giovanni 275

    Elisabetta Angela

    (Remondini) 275

Bertolini, Antonio 272

Berutti, Maria (Henrico)

    334, 336

Berutto, Martino 296

Bessola, Maria Angela

(Grosso) 298

Bettasso, Margaret

(Menghini) 305

Betty (Jackson) 324

Bezutti, Antonio 333

Carlo 323, 333

Francesca (Zanotti)

329, 333

Guiseppe 333

Biada, Margerita

(Giovanini) 250

Bise (Bubnar) 320

Bode, Lee Ann 306

Margie Lee (Flor) 306

Jim 306

Vernon Raymond 306

Boeger, Bertha Pauline

(Stefan) 258

Jacqueline Randina
(Figenschau) 259

William Frederick 258

Bohac, George R. 311

George R. Jr. 311

Bonato, Daniela (Fridle) 298

Bonatto, Anna Maria 325

Carlo Marchello 302 325

Catterina

(Malvassora) 325

Domenica (Coltro)

169 325

Marchello 169

Palmera (Alrasti) 325

Severino 325

Teresa (Dose) 325

Teresina (Da) 325

Bonino, Albert James 307-308

Angelina (Flor) 174

(pic) 305

Ashley 307

Bernard James 307

David George 308

Eda Tracilla 308

Edward John 307

Eugene E. 307

Giovanni Matteo 302

James 307

Louis (1899) 309

Luigi (Louis 1857) 86-89
168-169, 174 (picture) 293

Mary 87 174 (picture) 305

Pearl E. (Satti) 306

Richard Edward 308

Rosa (Tinetti) 86 88 166 168
170, 174 (pic) 179-180,
237-238

William Lawrence 308

Bottes, Bartolomeo 254

    Catharina (Stefani) 253

Bradbury, Susan Ellen

    (Gould) 260

Brizzolari, Charline Pearl

    Dexter) 269

Brogan, Curtis O. 318

Daniel Clair 318

Denise (Whitford) 318

James 318

James William 318

Janice L. (Morin) 318

Lynette 318

Orville Clair 318

Norine L. (Faircloth) 318

Rhonda J. (Smith) 318

Brooks, Janene L. (Jackson) 324

Brown, Ira L. 258

    Nellie Elizabeth (Stefan)
    115 177-178 258

Brownlee, Ethel Maude
    (Lemen) 261

Brunke, Carol S. (Peretti) 315

    Virginia Mae (Bryson) 315

    Walter Emmett 315

Bryson, Virginia Mae
    (Brunke) 315

Bubnar, Bailey 319

Betty Jane 319

Caleb 319

Dennis Clair 319

Edward James 316

Edward John 318

Gertrude A. (Baker) 320

Helen Ruth (Leman) 320

Ina Jessie (Harkness) 317

Ina Mable

(Madderom) 317

Bubnar, Isabelle 319

John 316

John 320

John Edward 320

John Robert 320

Juliette 319

Lori B. (Jackson)

Lorraine (Little) 320

Lynda Lee (Cox)

(Fitzhugh) 319

Matthew 319

Megan 319

Pearl Edna (Brogan) 318

Susan Jacqueline

(Bates) 319

Terri 319

Tyson E. 319

Burk, Katharine Lynette

Burr 309

Othie Glen 309

Burr, Albert James 309

Edward Glen 309

Katharine Lynette

(Burk) 309

Louis Earl 309

William Earl 308

William Edward 309

Byrnes, Catherine "Kay"

(Peretti) 323

John 323

C

Campi, Anna Maria

    (Olmari) 280

Campi, Giovanni Battista 280

Canesi, Margarita Maria

    (Olmar) 280

Cape, Lorraine Gayle

    Brogan) 318

Caposey, Alvera (Wasily) 314

Carli, Aiiana (Fridle) 288

    Francesco 288

    Luca 288

    Orsola (Wegher) 274

Catterina (Melchiori) 281 283

Catterina (Pastore) 333

Chini, Clara (Franchetti) 282

Churchill, Ronald C. 317

    Judith Ann

    Madderom) 318

Clark, Ann Florine (O'Neil) 267

    Margaret J. (Stefani) 261

Maurice Paul 267

Cohen, Christine Valerie (Kells)

    Ronald 268

    Sean M. 268

Coltro, Anna Maria 325

    Camilla 325

    Catterina (Malvassora) 325

    Giovanni 325

    Luca 325

    Luigi 325

    Maria Teresa (Reineri) 325

    Marco 188 191 214 (pic)

    215 219-221 325

    Teresa (Dose) 325

    Teresina (Da) 325

Conci, Alessandro Angelo

    Fortunato 287

    Anna Domenica

    (Angeli) 286

    Anna Maria Domenica (

    Piaz) 286

Francesco Antonio
Paoli 286

Giovanni Paolo 286

Guiseppe Luigi 286

Maria Catterina 287

Maria Domenica
Maddalena (Stefani) 41
53, 286 287

Nicola Ignacio 286

Conto, Teresa Emilia
(Tinetti) 298

Corder, Phil 306

Pearl (Bode) 306

Coss, Caroline (Miller) 260

Coppolla (de), Maria
(Tinetti) 295

Pietro 295

Cox, James D. 319

Lynda Lee (Bubnar) 319

Criscione, Angela Marie
(Weber) 271

Cristan (de), Andrea 279-280

Barbara (Olmari) 279

Giovanni 255

Giovanni Antonio 254

Irma (Fridle) 288

Maria Domenica
(Stefani) 255

Maria Maddalena
(Stefani) 254

Cromp, Amy (Henson) 311

Cromp, Daniel Joseph 311

Edwin 311

Jeffrey 311

Lynn (Pampuch) 311

Crosby, David Giles 262

Cuffaso, Domenico 299

Maddalena 299

Maria (Tinetti) 299

Curso, Andreas 335

Curtis, Kimberly A.
(Brogan) 318

Cussio, Antonio 337

Augusto Martino 334

Celeste (Celsetina) (Zanotti)

 331 335

Giacomo Antonio 331 334

Guiseppe 331

Helena Magdalena

(Fantino) 335

Maria (Zanotti) 334

Maria Margherita 335

Maria Rosa 334

Maria Teresa 169 300

331 335

Martino 334

Pietro Antonio 334

Rosa 335

D

Da (Bonatto) 325

Paolo 325

Da, Teresina (Bonatto) 325

Dale, Lester Edmond 260

Dallago, Barbara (Zoanetti) 255

Bartolo 255

Catherine Ellena 255

Cristano 255

Margarita (Stefani) 255

Davenport, Donald 268

Davis, James Albert Jr. 265

Virginia Mae (Holt) 265

Degani, Ellen J. (Jackson) 324

Michael L. 324

Dellachiale, Brian Arthur 324

Frank 324

Della Val, Giovanni 252

Maria Maddalena

(Stefani) 252

De Lorm, Roger M. 260

Derrick, Ted 321

Dever, Marian Frances 265

Dexter, Charline Pearl

(Brizzolari) 269

JoAnne (Kells) 269

Divigili, Alessia 289

    Cristian 289

    Disma 289

    Gabriella (Rigotti) 289

    Ivan 289

Dobas, Susanna (Bubnar) 320

Domenica (Friedle) 257

Domenica (Stefani) 249

Dorner, Andrew 262

    Frank Carl 262

    Bertha (Radkte) 262

Dose, Arena 325

    Paola 325

    Teresa (Bonatto) 325

Douthitt, Elizabeth

    (McGoldrick) 308

    Helen Cecilia

    (Bonino) 308

    James Perry 308

DuBois, Beth Aileen (Kells) 269

    David 269

    Mark William 269

    Mary Ellen 269

    Steven 269

    William H. 269

Duncan, Betty Jean (Peretti) 313

    Isabella (Kells) 267

    Joseph W. 313

Durkee, Floyd Allen 263

    Harmony M. (Adams) 263

    Stella (Peck) 263

E

Ebeling, Gloria June

    (Benning) 322

Eccher, Agata (Wegher) 272

Emanuel, Anita Mae (Holt) 264

    Carl Frank 265

    Eric 114 (pic) 116 264

    Mary Victoria (Stefani)

    104 104 (pic), 110 (pic)

    114 (pic) 116 264

Emright, Winifred
(Harkness) 317

Endrizzi, Pasqua
(Remondini) 27

Endsley, Eric James 265

George Russel 264

Helen Louise
(Rasmussen) 264

Mark Fleming 264

Merna Mae (Holt) 264

Russel Peter (Pete) 264

Ryan Michael 264

England, Eugene E. 307

Imogene (Bonino) 307

Ersdotter, Anna Louisa 264

Evangeline (Johnson) 263

F

Facchini, Elisabetta (Wegher) 41
55 272 287

Giacomo (1735) 287

Giacomo (1760) 272 287

Guiseppe Battista 287

Faircloth, Norine L.
(Brogan) 318

Tan F. 318

Faletti, Antonio 301

Giovanni Domenico 301

Maria (Favero) 301

Maria Teresa Emilia
(Tinetti) 301

Fantino, Domenico 336

Helen Magdalena (
Cussio) 335

Favero, Maria (Faletti) 301

Ferrando, Teresa (Tinetti) 298

Figenschau, Josephine Randina
(Boeger) 259

Finotti, Alessandra
(Mantovan) 288

Doriano 288

Sara (Stefano) 288

Tiziana (Fridle) 288

Fitzhugh, Lynda Lee

    (Bubnar) 319

    Mike 319

Fleckenstein, Douglas A. 260

    Marissa N.

    (Goldenman) 260

    Flor, Angelina (Bonino)

      174 (pic) 179-180 305

    Cesere 305

    James Angelo 305

    Jess Angelo 305

    Louis Jess 305

    Margie Lee (Bode) 306

    Ruth Ann (Marcotte) 305

Foerst, Lydia E. 268

Formolo, Giovanni254

    Lucia Maria 278

Forrester, Lucy Mae

    (England) 307

Fortenberry, Thomas 321

Francesca (di Olmar) 279

Franchetti, Anna Catherina 282

    Barbara Catterina
    Margareta 276 282

    Clara (Chini) 282

    Federico 281

    Giacomo Guiseppe 282

    Giacomo Michele 282

    Giovanni Domenico 281

    Giovanni Frederico

    (1685) 282

    Giovanni Frederico (

    1693) 282

    Guiseppe 41

    Guiseppe Antonio 282

    Margareta 41

    Margareta Barbara

    (Remondini) 276 282

    Maria Catterina 281

    Michele 281

    Franchi, Alice 288

Gemma (Fridle) 288

Mario 288

Martino 288

Matteo 288

Violante 288

Franzoi, Anna (Wegher) 273

    Teresa

    (Remondini) 278

    Giovanni Battista 280

Franzoi, Itala (Friedle) 257 288

    Lorenzo 273

    Margareta 274

    Stefano 280

Frej, Catterina (Pastore) 327

    Giovanni 327

    Guiseppe 327

Fridle(Friedel etc.)

    Anna (Kluiber) 291

    Anonimo 289

    Antonimo 257

    Ariana (Carli) 288

Augostino 290

Bianca Maria 257 289

Carmello 288

Daniela (Bonato) 288

Guiseppina Antonia

Odorizzi) 257

Irma (Cristan) 288

Martin 290

Nicole 290

Onorio Guiseppe 257 290

Orazio Firmo Luigi

257 290

Peter 290

Pietro 257

Suzy 290

Tiziana (Finotti) 288

Fridle, Vittorio (1918) 288

    Vittorio (1946) 216 223

    288 222 (pic)

G

Gabrieli, Giacomo 278

    Teresa (Remondini) 278

Gaunt, Donna Mae (Sanford)

    (Hart) 312

Genta, Cattarina (Zanotti) 329

Geosda, Maddalena

    (Cuffaso) 299

Gerhart, Donna Kay (Minix)315

    Michael Tad 315

    Michelle Lynn

    (Peretti) 315

Ghigo, Bernardo "Barney" 306

    Clara (Bonino) 307

Giblin, Margaret "Pearl"

    (Peretti) 318

Gin, see Maria Teresa Emilia

    Tinetti

Giovanna (Stefani) 32 249

Giovanni, Catterina

    (Stefani) 250

Giovanini, Giovanni 250

    Giovanni Battista 250

    Margarita (Biada) 250

Giustat, Maria Domenica

    (Bonino) 302

Goldenman, Marissa N.

    Fleckenstein) 261

    Peggy Jean (Lemen) 261

    Philip Samuel 261

Gomez, Edward 265

Gough, Charles Major 306

    Charles Major Jr. 306

    Charles Michael 306

    Clarence L. 306

Gould, H. Lester 260

    Harry Lester

    Morehead 260

    Susan Ellen

    (Bradbury) 260

Grace (McDermott) 323

Grosso, Antonia (Tinetti) 297

Antonio 297-298

Maria Angela

(Bessola) 298

Graziani, Giovanni 284

(Magnani) 284

Guicidati, Maria (Pastore) 326

Gruber, Katharine "Kate"

Peretti) 313

George August 313

Gualandi, Bartolomeo Adelmo

"Delmo" 312

Gualandi, Satimo "Sam" 312

Guglielmetti, Antonio 296

Maria (Tinetti) 296

Guilfoyle, Michael 324

Gutteridge, LaVerne 270

Charles 312

H

Hammond, Daniel Kenneth 266

Gary Lee 266

Gordon Kenneth 266

Gregory Charles 266

Kenneth Lee 266

Lawrence Sylvester 266

Lisa M Studley 266

Hammond, Marian Mae

(Stefani) 266

Hanson, William, Rev. 176

Harkness, Ina Jessie

(Bubnar) 317

James 317

John Emright 317

Harrison, Lola Mae (Little) 320

Hart, Carleton Wells, Jr. 312

Christine Ann 312

Donnamae Gaunt

(Sanford) 312

Madonna Rae

(Kessler) 312

Hemphill, Pearl (Pedersen) 260

Henrico, Domenico 336

Maria (Berutti) 334

Maria (Berutto) 336

Pietro 336

Henson (Cromp) 311

Herr, Constance Frances

(Lucenti) 311

Floyd Glen 311

Shirley Diane

(Koerner) 311

Hiatt, Geoffrey D. 265

Victoria Ann "Vicki"

(Holt) 265

Hickey, Harold 315

Judith Ann (Peretti) 315

Regina 315

Hoeuing, Ann (Hornung) 269

Hofer, Andreas 46 52

Hold, Jenny Victoria 264

Holt, Andrew C. 265

Anita Mae (Emanuel) 264

Anthony J. 265

Holt, Charles Edward, Sr. 264

Charles Edwin 264

Linda J. Maguire 265

Merna Mae (Endsley) 264

Merry Lee (Quy) 265

Sharon (Johnson) 265

Victoria Ann"Vicki"

(Gomez) (Hiatt) 265

William Charles 265

Hornung, Alfred 269

Samuel 269

Anna (Hoeuing) 269

Howard, Flossie A. (Prater) 315

Howell, Betty Sue (Prater) 314

Lloyd Ferald 314

Mary Evadine (Alvis) 314

Hudson, Elizabeth

Peterson) 270

Hunsacker, Lori Ann 269

J

Jackson, Albert L. 324

Arthur C. 321

Arthur William 324

Betty (?) 324

Diane (Dellachiale) 324

Frank L. 324

Frank William 324

Lois Ruth (Guilfoyle) 324

Lori B. (Bubnar) 319

Tim 319

John, Beatrice Ester

(Medrow) 320

Johnson, Delores (Quy) 265

Sharon (Holt) 265

(Smith) 322

Johnston, Edward 263

Edwina Joy 263

Evangeline 263

Karen Sue 263

Jones, Alice Caroline

(McClain) 321

K

Kane, Mary (Byrnes) 322

Katharine G. (Gough) 306

Kells, Beth Aileen (DuBois) 269

Christina Valerie

(Cohen) 268

Doris Muriel

Hornung) 269

JoAnne (Dexter) 269

Barbara (Wright) 267

Kathleen E. (Curtis) 268

Lawrence Carlisle 268

Lucas Carlisle 114 (pic)

116 267

Leila Stefani

(Newcomb) 268

Lyman Francis 267

Margaret Edith (Peterson) 122 (pic)124 133 144 (pic) 269

Milton Carlisle 268

Stephen Avery 267

Kessler, Benjamin Charles 312

Benjamin James 309

Benjamin Leroy 312

Hildegard (Koerner) 310

Joseph 309

Katharine Louise (Gualandi) 312

Madonna Rae (Hart) 312

Kirby, Charles 191

Virginia 191 211

Kluiber,Albert 291

Ann (Fridle) 291

Doris 290

Patrizia 290

Knock, Eloise Margaret (Negley) 270

Knowlton, Arthur Daniel 318

Clara Lee (Bubnar) 318

Koerner,David 310

Deanna 310

Debbie 310

Donald Benjamin 310

Donald Eugene 310

Hildegard (Kessler) 310

Kim 310

Linda 310

Mark 310

Marlene (Bohac) 311

Shirley Diane (Herr) 311

Steven310

Terri 310

Kollama, Cattarina 274

Krista (Adams) 264

L

Latt, Jenny Victoria 264

Lavalle, Gerald 323

Karen A. (Benning) 323

Lemen, Cecil LeRoy 261

Edwin Lionel 320

Ethel Maude

(Brownlee) 261

Helen Ruth (Bubnar) 320

James Gibson 261

Mary Luvina (Stuck) 320

Peggy Jean

(Goldenman) 261

Lewis, Austin Loren 322

Lightseg, Marybell

(Koerner) 312

Little, Buford Cecil 320

Buford Cecil Jr. 320

Edward M. 321

Laura (Little) 321

Lola Mae (Harrison) 320

Lorraine (Bubnar) 320

Ronald Buford 321

Sandra (Fortenberry) 321

Suzanne (Derrick) 321

Loner, Fulvia (Rigotti) 289

Long, Bertha Ellen

(Ammerman) 259

Lucenti, Constance Frances

Herr) 311

Lucia (Pastore) 326

Lucy (Chigo) 306

M

Madderom, Douglas John 317

Ina Mable (Bubnar) 317

John C. 317

Judith Ann

(Churchill) 318

Sydney Henry 317

Magnani, Ann 285

Barbara (Magnani) 285

Barbara (1681) 285

Barbara (1693) 285

Francesco 284

Giacoma 285

Giovanni 284

Giovanni Michele 28

Marco 282 284-285

Maria 284

Maria Magdalena 282 285

Michele 284

Pietro 285

Ursula 285

Ursula (Graziani) 284

Valentino 284

Maguire, Linda J. (Holt) 265

Maines, Bartolomeo 251

Malvassora,Catterina

    Bonatto) 325

    Elsa 325

    Luigi 325

    Piercarlo 326

Mantovan, Alessandria

    (Finotti) 288

    Fabrizio 288

Giacomo 289

Guilia 288

Marcotte, Joseph Bernard Jr. 305

    Ruth Ann (Flor) 89 305

Maria (de Olmari) (1645) 279

Marta, Battista 328

    Francisco 327

    Lorenzo 328

    Margerita (Pricco) 299

    Marta (Motto) 326

Martin, Lena Irene

    (Knowlton) 318

Martinetto, Antonio 326

    Maria (Pastore) 326

Mary Ellen (DuBois) 269

Mason, Beulah (Satterlee) 262

Mattevi, Guiseppina (Fridle) 289

    Ivo 289

    Luca 289

    Sylvia 289

    Sylvio 289

Ugo 289

Walter 289

Mayme (Duncan) 313-314

McClain, Alice Caroline

(Jones 321

Wallace Herbert 321

Walter Simms Hugh 321

McDermott, Barbara Jean

(Peretti) 323

Grace (McDermott) 323

William 323

McDonald, Arthur Leon

"Mac" 270

Leon Francis 270

Margaret Edith (Kells
(Peterson) 270

McElroy, Alexander John 312

Annie S. (McNamara) 312

Josephine Ione

(Koerner) 312

McGoldrick, Elizabeth

Douthitt) 308

McNamara, Annie S.

(McElroy) 312

Medrow, Arthur 320

Jane Elizabeth

(Peretti) 320

Melchiori, Antonio 283

Bartolomeo 283

Catterina (Melchiori)

281 283

Catterina (1662) 283

Daniele 283

Giacomo 283

Margareta 281

Margareta

(Franchetti) 284

Melchior 283

Melchiorius 281 28

Tomas Pietro 281

Menghini, Clementina 305

Edwino 305

Effie Mary (Flor) 395

Margaret (Bettasso) 305

Miller, Caroline (Coss) 260

Charles Fremont 260

Myron Charles 260

Milligan, Elizabeth F.
(Wedeking) 308

Minix, Donna Kaye

(Gerhart) 315

Monari, Domenica

(Facchini) 273

Moresco, Catterina

(Moresco) 274

Giovanni 274

Teresa 274

Moreta, Teresa (Tinetti) 296

Moriani, Domenica

(Facchini) 287

Giacomo 287

Morin, Gary Robert 318

Janice L. (Brogan) 318

Motto, Giovanna (Pastore)293

328 326

Guiseppe 326 328

Marta (Motto) 326 328

Martino 328

N

Nardelli, Francesco

Giovanni 255

Catterina Barbara

(Stefani) 255

Negley, Dennis Michael 270

Devin Margaret 271

Eloise Margaret

(Knock) 270

James Casper 270

Sean Marshall 271

Wendy Leigh

(Peterson) 270

Newcomb, Apollo 268

Aurora 268

Charles M. "Carlos" 268

Elena Anastasia 268

Jason 268

Jennifer B. 268

Leila Stefani (Kells) 268

Nichols, Rebecca Lynn

    (Adams) 263

Nilsdotter, Karina

    (Benning) 322

Noble, Gene 315

    Teresa Jean (Peretti) 315

O

Odorizzi, Enrico 290

    Guiseppina Antonia

    Friedle) 257 290

    Maddalena

    (Valentini) 290

Olmar (di Olmari, Volmar,

    Olmari)

    Anna 280

    Anna Maria (Campi) 280

Antonio 279

Barbara (1670)

(Franzoi) 280

Barbara (Cristan) 279

Barbara Magdalena 280

Cattarina (Remondini)

275 280

Christophel 279

Christoforos (1631) 280

Christophorous

(1665) 280

Francesca (Olmar) 279

Giovanni Battista 279

Innocente Giacomo 279

Margarita Domenica 281

Margarita Maria (Canesi)

Maria (Olmar) 279

Pietro (1550) 279

Pietro (1576) 279

Pietro (1632) 280

O'Neil, Ann Florine (Clark) 267

Oscari, Fortunata (Friedle) 257

P

Paizzardi, Liliargareta

    (Franzoi) 273

Pampuch (Cromp) 311

    Lynn (Cromp) 311

Parolini, Guidetta

    (Stefani) 254

Parrish Witt, Edgar Lewis 307

    Maytie Theresa

    Bonino) 307

Pastore, Antonino 326

    Bartolomeo 320

    Cattarina (1730)

    (Pastore) 333

    Catterina (1792) 327

    Catterina (1794)

    (Frej) 327

    Domenica (1753)

    (Zanotti)

330 333

Domenica (1795)

(Bellardi) 327

Domenico Antonio

Matteo 326

Eusebio 333

Giovanna (Motto) 293

326 328

Giuliana (Marta) 328

Lucia (Pastore) 326

Margherita 327

Maria (Guicidati) 326

Maria (Martinetto) 326

Maria Magdalena 155

161 298

Maria Magdalena

(Tinetti) 155 327 328

Marta (Sissoldi-Carlin)

(Marta) 327

Pietro Antonio 326

Simon 330 333

Patterson, Lee Eric 314

Pauline Marion (Kessler) 309

Peck, Stella (Durkee) 263

Pederson, Judith E.

    Ammerman) 260

    Henry P. 260

    Pearl (Hemphill) 260

Pence, Linda S. (Benning) 323

Peretti, Allafair (Prater) 315

    Alma Elizabeth

    (Jackson) 324

    Arthur 314

    Becky 316

    Betty Sue (Howell) 314

    Caloe 315

    Charles Guido 313

    Carol S. (Brunke) 315

    Catherine "Kate"

    (Gruber) 313

    Edith (Bubnar) 320

    Eugene 316

Eugene Leroy 316

Florence 316

Giovanni Battista 309

Holly (Ricca) 316

Jackie 316

James Edward 313

James R. 315

James Romeo 313

Jane Elizabeth (Medrow)

320

Jerry 316

Jessie Marie (Bubnar) 316

John Albert 313

John Michael, Jr 315

John Michael, Sr 315

Judith Ann (Hickey) 315

Katharine "Kate"

(Kessler) 309

Kimberly Marie 315

Louis Andrew 323

Louis V. 323

Margaret "Pearl"
(Giblin) 318

Michelle Lynn
(Gerhart) 315

Minnie see Tinetti, Maria
Teresa Domenica

Minnie"(Peretti)

Minnie Theresa (Smith)
(Benning) 321

Pamela M. 316

Peter 313

Pietro Giovanni (Peter)
302 309

Renee Jean 313

Robert Charles 313

Ronald George 314

Ronald George Jr. 314

Ronald George III 314

Maria Teresa Domenica
"Minnie" (Tinetti) 88 168
170 179-180 302-309

Teresa Jean (Noble) 315

William Anthony 315

Peterson, Alva Ola 259

Benson Ezra 259

Bertha Ann (Benson) 259

Carol Ann 259

Elizabeth (Hudson) 269

John Marshall 269

Margaret Edith (Kells)
(McDonald) 122 (pic)
124 133 144(pic) 269

Rhonda G. 269

Walter Leonard 269

Wendy Leigh
(Negley) 269

Petrini, Giuseppa Basso
(Tinetti) 300

Pietro 300

Pezzi, Margherita (Bezutti)
329 333

Pietro, Pietro 296

Prater, Flossie A. (Howard) 315

    Loss 315

    Vonda Gay

    (Wireman) 315

Preto, Giovanni 167

    Giovanni Martino

    300-301

    Pietro 301

Prieto, Marta (Tinetti) 299

Pricco, Antonio 299

    Giovanni 299

    Margarita (Marta) 299

Prine, Chloe (Jackson) 324

Q

Quy, Cheryl Lynn

    (Sucharski) 265

    Delores (Johnson) 265

    Harvey F. 265

    Lori Ann (Hunsacker) 265

    Merry Lee (Holt) 265

    Richard 265

    Scott 265

R

Radkre, Bertha (Dorner) 262

Rasmussen, Helen Louise

    (Endsley) 264

Regina (Hickey) 315

Reineri, Maria Teresa

    (Coltro) 215

Remondini, Anna Maria

    (1701) 275

    Anna Maria (1724) 275

    Cristofero 41, 276

    Claudia Teresa

    (Franzoi) 278

    Domenica Catterina 276

    Elisabetta Angela

    Berotto) 275

    Giacomo Antonio 276

    Gioseffa Francesca Maria

(Betta) 274

Giovanna Pietro 277

Giovanni (1698) 275

Giovanni (1766) 277

Giovanni (1784) 278

Giovanni Antonio 277

Giovanni Battista

(1731) 276

Giovanni Battista

(1820) 278

Giovanni Cristoforo

Antonio (1725) 276

Giovanni Cristoforo
Antonio (1757) 277

Guiseppe Germalius 276

Juliano Giovanni

Battista 276

Luigi Giovanni 275

Margareta Barbara

(Franchetti) 276 282

Maria Cattarina

(1759) 277

Maria Cattarina

1761) 277

Maria Catterina (1766)

(Stefani) 52-53 255 277

Maria Cristina (1766) 277

Maria Cristina (1768) 277

Maria Elisabetta 276

Monica (Wegher)16 79 87

88 206-207 211-212

234 (pic) 235 274

Sebastiano 277

Teresa (Gabriela) 278

Ricca, Ceyde 316

Holly (Peretti) 316

Michael 316

Rikki 316

Richards, Irene Anna (Burk) 309

Rigotti, Angelo 289

Daria (Fridle) 289

Fulvia (Loner) 289

Gabriella (Divigili) 289

Maddalena (Stefani) 254

Valentina 289

Valerio 289

Risdon, Barbara Ellen

(Hampton) 266

Daniel 266

Helen J. (Hammond) 266

Romans, Christine (Peretti) 315

Romanzak, Roseann Evelyn

(Noble) 315

Romlia, Catterina

(Franchetti) 281

Rossino, Lucia (Cussio) 314

S

Sallee, Frances Ellen

(Adams) 262

Sanford, Donna Mae

(Gaunt) 312

Satterlee, Beulah (Mason) 262

Clarence 262

Dawn (Adams) 262

Satti, Albert Preto 306

Janice (Gough) 306

Pearl E. (Corder) 306

Pearl E. (Bonino) 306

Schett, Annie (Gruber) 313

Schubert, Nevalyn M.

Adama) 262

De Scoppolla, Maria

(Tinetti) 295

Scovil, Leila (Wright) 267

Sento, Domenico 299

Rosa (Tinetti) 299

Sgarbossa, Dolores (Fridle) 290

(?) (Fridle) 290

Mattia 296

Mauro 290

Sharp, Laura Ann (Witt) 307

Sheehan, Kathleen Mary

(Kells) 268

Raymond Edward 268

Silva, Maddalena (Preto) 301

Simone (Franchi) 288

Sissoldi-Carlin, Antonio 327

    Marta (Pastore) 327

Smiley, LeVon F. 260

Smith, Allison L. (Johnson) 322

    Barbara Ann

    (Lewis) 322

    Delores Frances

      (McClain) 321

    Frederic Leland 318

    John Francis 321

    John J. 322

    Minnie Theresa

    (Peretti) 321

    Rhonda J. (Brogan) 318

    Terry Lynn (Little) 321

Snyder, Harlan M. 260

Starke, Alan 267-268

    Barbara Scovil (Wright)

267-268

Stefan, Arthur Frederick 114

    (pic) 116 258

    Bernice Jean "Babe"

    Leman) 261

    Dorothy Marie (Peterson)

    114 (pic) 259

    Elizabeth Josephine

    (Collatos) 259

    Frederick Frank (see also

    Stefani) 97 108, 114 (pic)

    186-187 258

    Jack Cushman 260

    John Frank 261

    Maxine Elizabeth

    (Ammerman) 114 (pic)

    178 259

    Nellie Elizabeth (Brown)

    114 (pic) 115 177-178 258

    Virginia Mae 114 (pic)

    178-179 188 260

Stefani, Adelaide (1717) 252

Adelaide Maria Anna 55
57 80

(pic) 216 223 257 288

Adelina Justina (Adams

(Dorner) 103 104(pic)

110 (pic), 114 (pic) 116

140 (pic)

261-262

Angelina Margherita

(Tinetti) 88-89 109 118

124-128 135 137, 141-

143 154 166 169-170

175-180 183-191, 195-

198 202 258 302 pics: 8

91 104 110 114, 122

140 174

Angela Carolina

Cattarina 254

Anna (1734) 251

Anna Maria

Margaretha 252

Antonia 251

Barbara Maddalena 256

Bartolomeo (1540)

31-32 249

Bartolomeo (1590) 249

Bartolomeo (1728) 253

Bartolomeo Antonio

Valentino 254

Catharina (Bottes) 253

Catharina (1688) (Di

Villa) 251

Catharina (1724) 254

Catterina Barbara

(Nardelli) 255

Catterina (Giovanni) 250

Clement Eugene 54 64 104

(pic) 110 (pic)114 (pic)

123, 124 140 (pic) 266

Daniele 252

Domenica

Clementina 256

Edith Rosetta (Kells) 47
103 104 (pic) 106 109 110
(pic) 111 114 (pic), 116
(pic) 122 (pic) 140 (pic)
194 (pic) 264

Ettore 228

Ferdinando 41 53 255

Ferrucio 216

Flore (Stefani) 31 250 279

Floriana 31 245

Francesco Antonio
Vigilio 253

Francesco Giovanni 63
66-72 79-82 85 258,
See also Frank

Francis Eugene George
104 266

Frank 15-16 57-58 63-72
77-82 89 103-110, 117-118
124-129 133-137 141-142
175 207, Pictures: 8 70 90

104 109 110 114 132 140
182 200

Stefani, Giacomo (1591) 250

Giacomo (1655) 250

Giacomo Antonio
Guidofalco 251

Giacomo Giovanni 55 257

Giovanna (Stefani) 32 249

Giovanni (1565) 31 249
250 279

Giovanni (1628) 250

Giovanni (1628) 250

Giovanni (1683) 251

Giovanni (1767) 52-
53 255

Giovanni Antonio 254

Giovanni Battista
(1559) 249

Giovanni Battista
(1628) 250

Giovanni Battista Antonio

(1695) 252

Giovanni Battista Antonio

(1725) 253

Giovanni Fortunato 254

Giovanni Giacomo

Maximilliano 254

Giovanni Francesco 57 see

also Frank Stefani,

Francesco Giovanni

Stefani

Giovanni Luigi 53-58 256

Giovanni Luigi

Ferdinando 55-58 64-

65 257

Girachino 254

Girachino Francesco 254

Girachino Giovanni

Antonio 254

Giudetta (Parolini) **254**

John Frank (1941) 98

103 267

Julio 253

Lucia 249

Luigia Maddalena 55-

56 258

Maddalena Catharina 254

Margaretta (1592) 250

Margarita (1790)

(Dallago) 255

Margaret J. 257

Maria (1589) (Olmar)

250 279

Maria (1622) 250

Maria Caterina

(Remondini) 52-53

255 277

Maria Domenica 252

Maria Domenica

(De Cristan) 255

Maria Domenica

Maddalena (Conci) 256

Maria Elizabetta 55 257

Maria Maddalena 253

Maria Magdalena

(Maines) 251

Maria Margaretha 251

Maria Margarita

Domenica 254

Marian Mae (Hampton)

47 122 (pic) 277 279 266

Mary Victoria (Emanuel)

104 116 264 pictures: 104,

114, 140

Peechie (Petje, Pietje)

(Bergsma) 65 123 179 266

Pietro Giovanni 255

Rina 227

Romedio 249

Stefano 255

Teresa Crescenza

Formolo) 254

Teresa Marianna 56 258

Tomas Antonio 253

Stefano (Finotti) 288

Stephany (Fridle) 290

Stuck, Mary Luvina

(Leman) 320

Studley, Daniel T. 266

Lisa M. (Hampton) 266

Stuve, Jaqueline Marie

(Adams) 262

Sucharski, Cheryl Lynn

(Quy) 265

Henry Fred 265

Kyle 265

T

Tenaglia, Catterina (Tinetti) 254

Testa, Denise 219Antonio

(1855) 298

Giovanni 303

Augustino 300

Guiseppa

(Guglielmetti) 303

Giusto Giovanni

Guiseppe 303

Italo 219

Thames, William Henry"Bill"

    237-238

Thompson, Patricia A.

    (Endsley) 264

Tinetti, Adele Seconda Maria

    Teresa 166 302

    Angela Domenica 296

    Angela Maria 297

    Angelina (1840) 300

    Angelina Margherita

    (Stefani)

    See Stefani, Angelina

    Margherita

    Angelo 298

    Anna Maria Marianna

    (Pricco) 299

    Antonia (Grosso) 297

    Antonio (1787) 295

Antonio (1816) 299

Antonio (1818) 299

Antonio (1821) 296

Antonio (1836) 298

Antonio (1838) 299

Antonio (1839) 299

Antonio (1855) 298

Antonio Amedio Secondo

162 167 168 170-171 300

Antonio Giovanni 299

Augostino 300

Benvenuto Federico 299

Catterina (Tenaglia) 254

Dionigi Pietro

Umberto 300

Domenica Felia

(Troselia) 295

Domenica (Pietro) 296

Domenica Maria 296

Domenica Maria

Teresa 300

Domenico (1779) 296

Domenico (1839) 297

Domenico
Bartolomeo 299

Florindo 300

Giacomo 154

Giovanna Antonia Maria
(Amosso) 154 296

Giovanna Maria (1783) 297

Giovanna Maria
1810) 299

Giovanni (1676) 295

Giovanni (1740) 296

Giovanni Battista 156
161-171 300 159-160 (pic)

Giovanni Pietro
Giacomo 300

Guiseppa Basso
(Petrini) 300

Guiseppe (1784) 155-
156 297

Guiseppe Antonio 297

Guiseppe Ottavio 162
167-168 300

Guiseppe Secondo
166 301

Joseph 300

Lorenzo Giacomo 298

Margherita 298

Maria Catterina 296

Maria (de Scoppolla) 295

Maria (Guglielmetti) 296

Maria Lucia 297

Maria Magdalena
(Pastore) 155 327-328

Maria Teresa 162 167 298
300-301

Maria Teresa Albina 166
169 191 302 325

Maria Teresa Domenica
"Minnie" 88 166 170
179-180, 302 309

Maria Teresa Emilia
(Falletti) 165 167 219
301 303

Maria Teresa
(Bonino) 166 168-169
179-180 302,
309 (picture)

Marta (Prieto)

Martino (1745) 154-155
295-296

Martino (1784) 296

Martino (1800) 297-298

Martino !1847) 298

Minnie (Peretti) see
Tinetti, Maria Teresa
Domenica

Michele 298

Pietro (1650) 154 295

Pietro (1707) 295

Pietro (1735) 295

Pietro (1783) 297

Pietro (1857) 298

Pietro Gioanni 298

Pietro Secondo 298

Rosie300

Still-born daughter
(1858) 301

Still-born daughter
(1859) 301

Teresa (Ferrando) 298

Teresa (Moreta) 296

Teresa Emilia (Conto) 298

Thomas 300

Virginia 165 301

Trosella, Domenica Felia
(Tinetti) 295

V

Valiante (Wright) 268

Valliere, Shannon Marie
(Dellachiale) 324

Valentini, Maddalena

(Odorizzi) 290

Van De Moere, Gail J.

    (Stefani) 267

Van Proyen, Marcia

    (Bubnar) 317

Venema, Harmke (Bergsma) 266

    De Villa, Carlos, 251

Vinson, June (Smith) 322

Vironda, Maria Catterina

    (Peretti) 302

Volmar, Pero 250

W

Wardas, Annie May

    (Cromp) 311

Wasiley, Alvera (Caposey) 314

    Anthony 314

    Deloris Deiane

    (Peretti) 314

Weber, Angela Marie

    (Criscione) 271

Crispin Lee 271

Devin Margaret (Negley)

Elinor Catharine 271

Elizabetta 256

Guiseppe 53-54 256

John Richard 271

Luigi 256

Maria Domenica

Maddalena (Conci)

    (Stefani) **53** 256 285-287

Maria Rose 256

Richard Lee 271

Wedeking, Elizabeth F.

    Milligan) 308

    Elizabeth Mary "Betty

    (Bonino) 308

    Harry L. 308

Wegher, Agata (Eccher) 272

    Alfonzo 86

    Agostino 272

    Anna (Franzoi) 273

Cecilia 272

Celeste Nicolo 274

Elisabetta (Facchini) 41 55
273 287

Elisabetta Maria Cattarina
(Stefani) 54, 256 274

Giacomo Giovanni 273

Gioseffa Francesca Maria
(Betta) 274

Giovanni (1738) 272

Giovanni (d. 1780) 272

Giovanni Antonio 272

Giovanni Francesco
1820) 273

 Giovanni Francesco
 (1821) 274

 Giovanni Luigi 273

 Giovanni Michele 274

 Giovanni Vincenzo 273

 Giulio 87-88 274

 Giulio Fortunato 88 274

Joseph J. 274

Josephine 274

Luigi Celeste 274

Luigi Paolino 41 55 273

Margareta (Bertolini) 272

Margareta (Wegher) 272

Maria (d. 1752) 272

Maria (d. 1781) 272

Maria Teresa 272

Michele (1710) 272

Michele (1768) 272

Monica Cunegonda
(Remondini) 16 79 87, 88
206-207 210 (pic) 211-212
234 (pic), 235 274 see also
Monica

Monica (1790) 272

Orsola (Carli) 274

Teresa Maria Luigia 274

Teresa (Zanon) 273

Virginia 274

Weir, Isabelle Maude 270

Whitford (Brogan) 218

Whittenberg, Pauline
(Degani) 324

Wicker, Mary Melissa
(Brown) 258

Witt, Laura Ann (Sharp) 307

Wireman, Andrea Yvonne
Peretti) 315

Ernst Rodeny 315

Jesse 315

Sherry M. (Peretti) 315

Vonda Gay (Prater) 315

Wolff, Lydia (Hampton) 266

Wright, Barbara Scovil (Kells)
(Starke) (Valiante) 267

Leila (Scovil) 267

Mark Hatfield 267

Wyma, Effie (Madderom) 317

Z

Zancanella, Catterina 274

Zanet, Elisabetta (Stefani) 251

Zanon, Teresa (Wegher) 273

Zanotti, Antonio (1784) 330

Antonio (1799) 331

Bartolomeo (1713) 329

Bartolomeo (1766) 329

Battista 330

Carlo 329 330

Carlo Antonio (1829) 332

Carlo Antonio (1833) 332

Carlo Antonio (1840) 331

Cattarina 330

Cattarina (Genta) 330

Celesta Maria 332

Clara Rosa 332

Domenica (Pastore)
330 333

Domenico (1628) 329

Domenico (1758) 334

Eusebio 329

Eusebio Giovanni 330

Francesca (1744) (Bezutti) 329 333

Francesca (1785) 330

Francesco 329

Giovanna Domenica

Lucia (Cussio) 331

Giovanni Antonio (1770) 330
Giovanni Antonio (1840) 331
Guiseppe 331

Margherita Maria 330

Maria Catterina 330

Maria Lissia 331

Maria Margherita 330

Maria Teresa 331

Pietro 329

Secondo 165 300 331

Simon 331

Zanotti-Cussio, Domenica Cattarina (Tinetti) 161-165 ,300 332
Maria Cattarina (Tinetti)

161-166 169, 170-171

301 332

Zeni, Maria (Stefani) 251

Zoanetti, Barbara (Dallego) 255

ABOUT THE AUTHOR

Wendy Negley was born in Chicago, Illinois and was raised far from her main family. When she moved to Seattle with her mother and sister, she met her Stefani family. Many years later knee deep in finding her family tree she discovered that the Mormon Library had microfilm copies of the church and civil records for her Stefani and Tinetti family towns in Italy. She spent over a year at her local Family History Library researching these records. Her family was not interested in hearing about it but they loved the stories, therefore she decided to write this book. She hopes that you enjoy it!

Please email her and let her know how you like it, any questions you may have and/or any corrections you might have (there can always be a revised edition!) Wendy would love to hear from you! Her email is wnegley@gmail.com. She also has a website: wendynegleypoet.com.

46 WENDY BETWEEN HER COUSINS VALENTINA AND VALERIO RIGOTTI AT
CASTEL SPOR NEAR SPORMINORE, ITALY **2014**